Where Was the Prodigal's Mother?

LEARNING TO TRUST HER SON TO THE FATHER

Sandra Kearns

CROSSBOOKS·
PUBLISHING

CrossBooks™
A Division of LifeWay
1663 Liberty Drive
Bloomington, IN 47403
www.crossbooks.com
Phone: 1-866-879-0502

First published by CrossBooks 6/14/2010

ISBN: 978-1-6150-7177-7 (sc)

Library of Congress Control Number: 2010925414

Printed in the United States of America
Bloomington, Indiana

This book is printed on acid-free paper.

Scripture taken from:
The Living Bible, Tyndale House Publishers, Wheaton, Illinois, 60187, Copyright© 1971.

The New Open Bible, Study Edition, Thomas Nelson Publishers, Copyright©, 1990, 1985, 1983 by Thomas Nelson, Inc., NKJV.

The Comparative Study Bible, A Parallel Bible, presenting the NIV, NAS, Amplified, King James versions. Copyright© 1984 by The Zondervan Corporation.

This book is dedicated to my family and friends who have supported and encouraged me through many difficult years.

Your prayers and words of comfort have undergirded me and given me the courage to step into each new day, with God's strength, to take life one day at a time.

I pray I will continue to persevere in the challenges of life.

When we are suffering, we need a friend to pray with and for us when we don't have the words to express our pain.

You have been there to do that.

I thank you each one.

Contents

"Take the very hardest thing in your life---the place of difficulty, outward or inward, and expect God to triumph gloriously in that very spot. Just there He can bring your soul into blossom!"[1]

Lilias Trotter

FORWARD

Our children can be a source of great pleasure or great pain depending largely on the choices they make. Few things bring more pain to parents than to see their children make destructive choices. Many of these choices are related to drugs and alcohol and some of these choices lead to criminal acts. Every day the media reports local arrests for large and small criminal offenses. Many of these crimes are drug related.

People who are under the influence of alcohol and drugs do things they would never do when they are sober. Drug abuse and its results are so common in our culture that we tend to see it as simply a sad reality, but it does not affect our lives very deeply unless it is our son or daughter who is arrested.

This book is written from the heart of a mother who has walked closely with God and with her prodigal son. She has made many visits to prison, answered many late night phone calls from authorities or from a son who was asking for help, but really wanted money for more drugs.

The author confesses that her source of strength has come from God and His earthly helpers. Friends and strangers have spoken words of hope and help. Various other authors have spoken insightful words to her heart in the darkness of night.

Where there is faith, there is hope. Where there is prayer, there is the listening ear of God. Patience is a virtue that grows as one waits for a prodigal to return. Here is the journey of an ordinary Christian who has had a large serving of pain and with the help of God has not only survived, but is now engaged in a ministry to other parents and spouses who have a family member who is incarcerated. She knows how to weep with those who weep and rejoice with those who rejoice.

You will not read this book without tears, but through the tears, you will also find help and hope.

Gary Chapman, author of The Five Love Languages and Love as a Way of Life

Gary is also the Associate Pastor of Calvary Baptist Church in Winston-Salem, N. C. where the author has attended church for twenty-six years.

INTRODUCTION

"In this you greatly rejoice, though now for a little while you may have had to suffer grief in all kinds of trials. These have come so that your faith—of greater worth than gold, which perishes even though refined by fire—may be proved genuine and may result in praise, glory and honor when Jesus Christ is revealed." I Peter 1:6-7 (NIV).

I stopped by my husband's place of employment the other week. He was deep in conversation with a man, so I stood back to let them finish their conversation. Shortly thereafter, Jimmy, my husband, called me over and introduced me to the gentleman. I discovered, after our introduction, that the conversation was about his son who was serving time in prison for DWI charges. It was not the son's first time being in trouble, and the father explained with deep hurt and sorrow in his voice that he had tried to help him so many times by providing lawyers and by paying off his debts, but to no avail. The young man continued down the path of destruction despite the father's efforts.

This father was still in the stages of letting go, where I had often found myself as I tried to help our prodigal son over the years. I explained to him that I was still learning to take my hands off and give my son into the hands of the Lord. The hardest prayer I ever prayed was, "Lord, do whatever it takes to open up his eyes and draw him to Yourself."

As I left that distraught father, I knew there were many other hurting parents who needed a word of encouragement, hope, and support. My prayer is that God will speak to your broken heart, if you find yourself in the position of this father, as I share what God has taught me over the years.

I am very aware that my trials may pale in comparison with some you may face. Each of us could probably write our own story, but I hope you find some encouragement from these words that come from my heart.

This is not a writing of how to's in living your life or raising your children. This is about my journey with the Lord through much hurt, pain, and sorrow of everyday life and how He brought me through to a closer relationship with Him.

There were some moments, I must confess, in the beginning of my journey that I doubted His presence. There were times when I was in such despair and had such a sense of hopelessness that I could not see Him in the circumstances of my life.

There was one particular moment I remember well as I sat on my front porch. I was crying out to God to show Himself to me because I could see no light at the end of the tunnel. I had no sooner spoken, when a dove flew down at my feet, so close I could almost reach out and touch it. I knew in my spirit it was a visual confirmation of His presence with me, and it gave me comfort and peace.

As Gideon asked for a sign in Judges 6, he knew it was a lack of faith and asked God not to be angry with him, but Gideon needed a confirmation at that point. God did not rebuke him but gave him what He asked to increase his faith. He knew what Gideon needed at that time in his life and provided clear direction through the visible sign. I am a visual learner, and God knew the appearance of the dove would bring me comfort. After all, the dove is representative of the Holy Spirit, and God said he would send the Comforter to dwell with us at His ascension. What a personal God we have who meets our every need!

I am not proposing that we ask God for signs at every turn but I believe He is not angry when we ask at confusing times in our lives for His direction or for His presence in a definite manner.

The dove has been very special to me ever since that day. I recognize the sound of a dove more clearly now, and it is a comfort to me. You might say, oh, that was just a coincidence that a dove flew down at that moment, but I know in my heart that God answered my heart's cry.

Prayer: Lord, I pray this book will bring comfort to the hurting hearts of families who have a prodigal who has chosen to

walk away from Your plan and purpose for their lives. Use the words in these writings to be a salve to hurting hearts. Please remove the blinders of our prodigals, and bring them home to Your dear self. We ask You to hurry Lord, Amen.

CHAPTER ONE

The Birth of Twins and Their Father's Wrong Choices!

"Instead of their shame my people will receive a *double portion*, and instead of disgrace they will rejoice in their inheritance; and so they will inherit a double portion in their land, and everlasting joy will be theirs." Isaiah 61: 7 (*Italics mine, NIV*).

I will begin my story with a very trying time in the life of our family and then back up to how God took me through other issues over the years. I will also share the times He taught me His provision as He called me on mission with Him, how He comforted me in times of tragedy, and gave me strength in times I knew I had none through His Word. You will see lots of references from which God gave me promises and hope to go on day by day, not only through the pain of a prodigal son but in other tragedies that would come my way. This will not be a perfect manuscript or maybe even what you expected but I pray it will help you in whatever circumstances you find yourself.

I am beginning to see some old signs of rebellion rearing its ugly head in our son, Robbie. He is staying out late and we are concerned with what he is doing during those hours since he has a history of drug and alcohol abuse. We have not seen much of him these past few days, and we are concerned. I am afraid he is traveling down the same path he has before. I pray to the Father to protect him and to draw him to Himself. Robbie must want this for himself, and right now he thinks he is still in control of his life.

Not long after I prayed about all this, Robbie came home one night with the announcement that his girlfriend, Tina, was pregnant. I wondered how much more I could take! This amplified the concern we had for Robbie in our hearts. We were worried about how he would be able to support a baby. As Christians we know that this is not God's perfect plan for starting a family. This is going to be a long hard road for all of them. Robbie sure doesn't need a family to be responsible for right now because he can't even be responsible for himself.

One day, as I was home from work doing some cleaning, the door bell rang, and there stood Tina asking for Robbie. He happened to be gone at the time, so I asked her what she needed, and she said she was on the way to have an abortion. Robbie had been very upset about her plan, telling her not to do it. I believe she was there because she really didn't want to follow through with it.

I told her she did not have an option, and if she carried through with her plan she would be killing our grandchild. I tried to encourage her to change her mind and told her we would support her in that decision if she chose to have the baby. As much as I did not like the news, I could not encourage anyone to abort a child. God's Word says, **"My frame was not hidden from you, when I was made in the secret place, when I was woven together in the depths of the earth, your eyes saw my unformed body. All the days ordained for me were written in your book, before one of them came to be." Psalm 139: 15-16 (NIV).** She listened and did not go for her appointment for which we are all most grateful.

Not long after I was reading the following words in Rick Warren's book, The Purpose Driven Life:

> "Regardless of the circumstances of your birth or who your parents are, God had a plan in creating you. It doesn't matter whether your parents were good, bad, or indifferent. God knew that those two individuals possessed exactly the right genetic makeup to create the custom 'you' he had in mind. They had the DNA God wanted to make you.

While there are illegitimate parents, there are no illegitimate children. Many children are unplanned by their parents, but they are not unplanned by God. God's purpose took into account human error, and even sin." [1]

I made the announcement of the baby to my prayer partners in our room where we prayed underneath the pulpit on Sunday mornings. We prayed together, and Joan, our leader, prayed that God would give me a double portion of blessing from the following scripture. **"Instead of their shame my people will receive a *double portion*, and instead of disgrace they will rejoice in their inheritance; and so they will inherit a double portion in their land, and everlasting joy will be theirs." Isaiah 61: 7,(*Italics mine,* NIV).**

The next week we found out the incredible news that we were having two babies. I went back the next week and jokingly commented to Joan that I knew God heard her prayers, but did she remember she had prayed for us to have a double portion and now we were having twins!

Robbie was with Tina at the hospital on the night the babies were born. First came Shelbi Lynn, then Carolyn Elizabeth. We went to the hospital to see them and found two very little babies in incubators. We were able to hold and feed them both and place a stuffed animal in the incubator with them. Rob seems to be very proud of the babies and is holding them and learning to change and feed them. Lord, is this what you will use to change his direction?

As I prepared to go to a musical being held at our church several nights later, the phone rang, and it was Robbie calling from the Rowan County jail. He and another guy were arrested for breaking and entering a house. He wanted me to get him out, saying he needed to be with his babies. I was infuriated as I listened to his story, so I told him he should have thought of that before and hung up the phone.

Lord, why is this happening again? I pray and pray for our son and the promises you have given me for him just don't ever seem in reach. I was so in hopes that these two little babies would get his attention. I turned to **Job 17: 15-16 (NAS)** which echoes my plea, **"Where now is my hope? And who regards my hope? Will it go down with me to Sheol? Shall we together go down into the dust?"** I know my hope is in the Lord, not in the circumstances, but it is so hard to understand why things happen as they do! Every time I think Robbie is headed in the right direction, all hope seems to be gone again.

I called one of my dear friends, Dee Dee, and heard this on her answering machine, "My hope is in the Lord Jesus." Thank you for that reminder, Lord. I needed to hear it again because all my hope seems to have vanished.

I have chosen not to receive any calls from Robbie. I even told my fellow employees that I did not have a son anymore. Wouldn't that make it easier? I came to the following passages, which brought me comfort:

Isaiah 43: 1b-2 (KJV), "Fear not, for I have redeemed you; I have called you by name; you are Mine! When you pass through the waters, I will be with you; and through the rivers, they will not overflow you. When you walk through the fire, you will not be scorched, nor will the flame burn you."

Psalm 34:18 (NAS), "The Lord is near to the brokenhearted and saves those who are crushed in spirit."

Psalm 27: 13-14 (NAS), "I would have despaired, unless I had believed that I would see the goodness of the Lord in the land of the living. Wait for the Lord; be strong, and let your heart take courage; yes, wait for the Lord."

II Corinthians 1: 3-4 (NIV), " Praise be to the God and Father of our Lord Jesus Christ, the Father of compassion and the God of all comfort, who comforts us in all our troubles, so that we can comfort those in any trouble, with the comfort we ourselves have received."

I wrote in my journal, "Help me trust in You at all times; help me to pour out my heart to You, God, for You are my refuge." This was my prayer as I read from Psalm 62:8.

Just when we thought matters could not get worse, it did. At 10:00 pm on a Monday night, we heard the doorbell ring, and upon opening the door we found four detectives with our son, who was dressed in an orange jumpsuit with handcuffs on his hands and shackles on his feet. We knew this couldn't be good. They came in and sat down on the couch on either side of Robbie and began to tell us that our son had been involved in several break-ins in our own neighborhood. He had cooperated with them in every way, but we knew he was in deep, deep trouble. As they continued to talk, one of the detectives expressed to us that our community was very tightly knit and would probably not be very forgiving of him or us.

In some respects we found this to be true. I saw neighbors in little huddles talking and looking up at our house. Most said nothing at all, but a few greeted us and expressed their sorrow for what we were experiencing. It was interesting to see how some responded to us. Some tended to blame us for his actions, choosing to no longer acknowledge us as they looked the other way. It hurt very badly, but I took it to the Lord and attempted not to be bitter toward them for their lack of compassion. I partially understood their reaction, but still grieved. I hoped one day they would be able to have complete forgiveness in their hearts.

May I interject at this point that when people are hurting that you not just pass them by for fear of not saying the right thing, or as I've heard so many times, "I didn't know what to say, so I felt it better to say nothing." Just tell the person you are praying for them, that you love them, or that you are so sorry they are going through the trial, but don't just ignore them. That hurts clear through to the heart. If nothing else, just put your hand on their shoulder, or if you feel comfortable hug them, but please don't say, "I understand", if you really don't. Some who didn't have a clue about the pain and heartache we felt have expressed those words to Jimmy and I. They meant well, but it was of no real comfort. If you haven't walked in the shoes, you cannot know how we felt. If you have, it is even more important that you try to minister as the Lord leads you.

Then again, there were some who were so forgiving even though they had been personally violated by our son. They were wounded and hurt but have continued the same relationship we always had with them. They even offered forgiveness to our son. Now those were true demonstrations of forgiveness. We will be eternally grateful to them for their kindness.

As the detectives talked, it seemed to be a big celebration for them to have cracked the case. They were joking and laughing like it was something they were enjoying, but as his parents, we were dying inside. I did not even want to look at our son who sat so pitifully on the couch. I was really angry and ashamed at this point, wondering how in the world we had gone so wrong as parents.

I did hug him as he was led out the door and told him I loved him, but at that moment I was very angry with him. I knew he had done himself in for a very long time, and honestly all hope vanished that I would ever see him serving the Lord in the way I hoped. I desired to see him becoming the man and the father for the girls he needed to be, and now he was off to prison for who knows how long.

Did I question God at this time? Yes. Why would He allow this to occur after all the prayers that we had lifted to Him in Robbie's behalf over the years? Why, when He had given me so many promises that He would bring him back from the enemy's territory? I don't understand, Lord. It looks so impossible now, even though I am often reminded that nothing is impossible with You. Oh Lord, teach me to trust you in all things.

Once again, I felt as if I have lost my son. Would death have been any more traumatic? Have I lost him to the enemy and the world anyway?

He has certainly been blinded and deceived by Satan, even after years of prayers to remove the blinders and to help him to see and hear from You Lord. It seems my hopes get lifted up each time just to be brought crashing down, each time spiraling farther downward.

I cried and cried until I was spent of tears. I continued to refuse any phone calls from Robbie, and for the first time I did not have a desire to talk to him. I just didn't even know what to say to him, and questioned if anything I said would make any difference anyway. It totally frustrated me.

The Lord is giving me strength to even get out of bed in the mornings. Who is this person in front of the mirror putting on make-up? Am I to go out and give hope and encouragement to others having surgery or dealing with life-threatening illnesses in light of how I am feeling? How many days have I crawled to work in distress over issues with our son?

I am leading a Bible Study and feel I must go because so many ladies are depending on me. Lord, help me to hold up and do what You would have me to do. I need Your strength and presence with me. Our daughter, Melissa, is attending the Bible Study, and it thrills my heart to see her growing in the Lord. This is my heart's desire for both of my children. I am reminded of **III John 1:4 (NAS), "I have no greater joy than this, to hear of my children walking in the truth."**

In days gone by I would not have even been able to talk about what was going on with our son without breaking down in tears and absolute grief. As I grow in the Lord I am slowly learning to lean on Him and to accomplish His will in my life regardless of my circumstances. As Jimmy arrives from work, I see the pain in his eyes and know he is hurting as badly as I am. We both look like we have aged so much, and our gastrointestinal tracts are overly active. It always seems to affect our whole system when we are going through this turmoil with our son. I literally feel like I might just lose it sometimes. Wouldn't that be easier, to just retreat into ourselves and block out the world?

I remember a patient I had in nursing school who was catatonic. I would sit with her, and she would never speak a word. She was always in her own little world. I used to wonder what had been so tragic in her mind to cause her to withdraw from everyone. How sad! But now I see how escape would be a safe place to be and why someone would want to withdraw.

The Lord does give me the strength to get to Bible Study because He knows I need it more than the others. It helps me so much to be in the Word and study it in depth. It is what keeps me sane.

I stayed up late one night cleaning up Rob's room and the downstairs family room. I rearranged the room and just tried to stay busy and work out the anger I felt. Again, it was like he has died and might not be coming back home. So sad to fold away his clothes knowing he won't need them for a long time.

It was hard to even set foot in the yard with the news of what our son did. It made me sick to my stomach and caused such pain. I felt as if everyone was talking about us and what bad parents we must be. I went out into the yard with my sunglasses and hat on hoping to avoid contact with anyone.

I met a dear friend at the local post office whom I don't see very often anymore. She hugged me and told me when she saw the newspapers that she wanted to buy them all up so that I wouldn't have to see them and so that no one else would either. How comforting it was to know that she loved us and wanted to protect us from the scandal. Her words were like a soothing balm to my hurting heart.

I am discovering a new empathy for those parents or loved ones I hear about on the news whose children or spouses have been incarcerated. It is a humiliating experience. I see the pain and agony in the faces of mothers and fathers, spouses and children as they visit with the inmates. I now know their pain and feel the agony of their hearts. It is a grieving process just as if he has died, because our hopes and dreams for him seem to have.

Robbie has not attempted to call us in a few days. Maybe he is angry with us for not accepting his calls, but he needs to reflect on his actions by himself right now. I hope he is very remorseful for what he has done. Lord, soften his heart. May he cry out to You in his solitude!

On the way to work, the Lord and I always talk about the day ahead, and I sing praises to Him. Today He speaks to my heart. "Have I ever disowned you----when you have disobeyed and sinned against Me?" No, He has given me chance after chance to mend our relationship and fellowship. He has shown me grace and mercy time and time again.

Rob is our child, always will be, no matter what he does. Even though our fellowship is broken for the time being, our relationship is forever. I love him very much and must remember to lift him up to the Father each day. I am reminded frequently of Henry Blackaby's words as he prayed with me at a seminar at The Cove, "Lord, help this Mother to never give up." That prayer came to mind often as the years progressed and it seemed it would be easier to give up.

"Consider it pure joy, my brothers whenever you face trials of many kinds, because you know that the testing of your faith develops perseverance. Perseverance must finish its work so that you may be mature and complete, not lacking anything," James 1:2-4 (NIV) states. I pray God will help me persevere. God is giving me more peace with each new day. Even though the circumstances are raging, my heart is at peace. My strength is coming from the Lord as I talk with Him and stay in His Word.

God is not shocked by the turn of events in our lives; He knew this all along. He will use this in Rob's life. I must not give up but continue to stand in the gap for him. I will not allow Satan to have him. God is not a liar; He keeps His promises. I would not have chosen this for Rob or for our family, but God's ways are not our ways, and we must trust He is doing a work in all of us.

A friend called to share Matthew 14:22-36 with me. Jesus put the disciples in the boat and sent them to the other side. He went up to the hills to pray. So…Jesus put us in the boat before this last storm. He knew what we would face. When the storm was raging around His disciples, they were afraid. He told them to take courage. I Am, so stop being afraid. When Peter walked out on the water and began to doubt and sink, Jesus immediately reached out His hand to save him from drowning. He got in the boat, and the wind ceased. I have felt much the same strength since that phone call. I knew Jesus had been in the boat with me all along, but I sensed it more clearly now. He is so faithful to us. I love Him so much, and I trust Him with my life and with my children's lives.

A little while later, we had a great visit with our new granddaughters when Tina brought them to see us. Carolyn has fat cheeks like Rob did as a baby. Shelbi has gained some weight but is still the smallest. Melissa, our daughter, and Debbie, a dear friend, came over, and we had a great time holding and kissing on them. We all gave gifts of clothes and diapers as we marveled at the miracle God had performed in bringing them into our lives. They seem to fill a void we now feel with the imprisonment of our son. I wonder how often we will be able to see them with the circumstances of their father as they are.

Prayer: Lord, you know we want to be a part of our grandchildren's lives and to grow them up in the nurture of the Lord Jesus Christ. I pray you will work in the heart of their mother so that the girls will be allowed to go to see their father and bond with him in the coming days. Help us to persevere in spite of the difficulties we face in order to bring glory to Your name, Amen.

CHAPTER TWO

Obedience to God Brings Peace

"If you love me, you will obey what I command. He who does not love me will not obey my teaching." John 14:15, 24, (NIV).

Now let me step back in time a bit to share where my journey had led me up to this point. Each chapter has been a learning experience with my Lord. It was a cold day in April, when my husband, Jimmy, and I started up the road to Blowing Rock, North Carolina. As we approached the foothills, the snow began falling gently on the windshield. As we drove farther up the mountain, the flakes began beating down on us even harder, almost as if someone were throwing them toward us. Looking ahead at the snow covered mountains the beauty of the scenery appeared to be a sign of God's favor on us as we preceded on our journey in an attempt to be obedient to God's call for me to write.

I was following what I believed to be the leading of the Lord to begin writing as He had directed me. He had been dealing with me for some time, and I suppose I had been dragging my feet, not unwilling, but not knowing how to begin. He had taught me so many times to just step out in faith and obey Him and He would provide all I needed. Why did I find this to be so difficult? Mainly because I wonder who in the world would want to read what I have to say!

I am reminded by the Lord that He used the mouth of the donkey in **Numbers 22: 28 (NIV), "Then the LORD opened the mouth of the donkey…"** Surely if He can put His words in the donkey's mouth, He can do the same with me. I trust Him to do just that as we head to the mountains.

This is my prayer from **Jeremiah 1:9 (NKJV), "Then the Lord put forth His hand and touched my mouth, and the Lord said to me, 'Behold, I have put my words in your mouth."** I know I can do nothing without Christ and He will supply the words I need.

Moses serves as a perfect example of my resistance to obey the Lord's calling. He argued with the Lord that he wasn't qualified to do what God had called him to do. In **Exodus 4:10 (AMP), "And Moses said to the Lord, 'O my Lord, I am not eloquent or a man of words, neither before nor since You have spoken to Your servant; for I am slow of speech, and have a heavy *and* awkward tongue.' "**

In verse fifteen God said, **"I will teach you"**. God promised to assist him in the new assignment He had for Moses. I believe Moses was coming way out of his comfort zone as he accepted the challenge. That is much the way I feel as I begin this new chapter of my journey, but I believe He will teach me as we walk together.

God says in **John 14:15 (NIV), "If you love me, you will obey what I command."** I want to experience everything He has for me, so my desire is to be obedient out of my love for the Father.

Several years ago, I felt the Lord call me out to do a new thing, but I couldn't get a grasp of what that was at the time. He kept saying He wanted me to stop what I was doing and come aside with Him and He would begin to show me what that would be.

At the time, I was leading a women's Bible study which I had begun at my place of employment seven years before. Several of the nurses would come when they got off duty to have a two-hour time of sharing their insights with each other from homework they had done the week before. The group began to grow as each one of them would invite others to join us. We started out studying <u>Experiencing God, Knowing and Doing the Will of God,</u> by Henry Blackaby and Claude V. King. The study literally changed my spiritual life and I went on to facilitate three more groups in that study.

We moved from the <u>Experiencing God</u> study to others, such as <u>The Vision of His Glory</u> written by Anne Graham Lotz, and most of the studies written by Beth Moore. I had such a passion to ignite the fire of the Lord in these ladies through continued Bible study and to help them realize God wanted an intimate relationship with them.

Facilitating each study became something comfortable for me. Once again, God began to speak to me about moving out of my comfort zone to begin a new work with Him. It was hard to just walk away from the ladies in the class. I began to ask the Lord to show me who could lead the women's Bible studies. He showed me a lady by the name of Kim who was already participating in our group. After praying, I approached Kim with the idea one evening, and after her own season of prayer, she accepted the call. To this day the ladies continue to meet regularly, and I praise the Father for His provision and that they continue to grow in the Lord

As I finished that final study, I began to ask the Father what He wanted me to do. After hearing of a trip planned by our church to send some folks to the Middle East, God showed me that I was to go on that trip, but I continued to feel restless in my pursuit of His will for my life. Upon receiving no clear direction, I was approached about beginning a Bible study by our teacher in my Bible Fellowship class, and I readily agreed to facilitate it. I was back in my comfort zone, but I knew it was not exactly what God intended. I continued to seek His face for direction.

The thought of writing my story came to me several times, but I quickly abandoned the idea. I felt very inadequate, and still do. Oftentimes I would sit down to write, but quickly felt frustrated and would give up but I could not shake the leading of the Holy Spirit to continue to put the words on paper.

Recently, God has placed on my heart the burden to write again but, I wanted to make sure it was of Him, so I began to listen closely for His voice. My friends had suggested many times that I write my experiences, but I continued to put it off. I suppose I was scared I couldn't do it and hesitant to relive the painful memories of my life.

I had accepted the Lord as my Savior at age eight. I sat on my little bunk bed with my Dad after church one Sunday night and asked Jesus into my heart. But I had not really understood until the <u>Experiencing God</u> by Henry Blackaby study that God wanted to have a personal relationship with me.

I had stayed pretty close to the Lord throughout my childhood through my involvement in many church activities, such as sword drills, Vacation Bible School, and Girls in Action. These activities taught me so much in my early days and helped ground me in the Word. I didn't realize at that time that the Word was alive and active. Many times while reading the Bible, I found I was bored, but that has all changed at this point in my life.

My Dad was called into the ministry when I was about nine or ten years of age. We lived on the east coast of North Carolina during my childhood years, and I learned to clam, to catch crabs on the dock with fatback and chicken necks, and to eat all kinds of seafood. That was a simpler life.

Being a preacher's kid in those days usually meant others judged you with a different set of rules. I felt many times as if we lived in a glass house where everyone could see our every move. Everyone seemed to judge us by their standards of how a preacher's family should act or react. The joke used to be that if the preacher's kids were bad it was because we played with the deacons' kids.

My Dad and Mother kept me in the Word through Bible study and church attendance, for which I am most grateful. Both of my parents were raised in broken homes due to alcohol. They were oftentimes separated from their parents and siblings as they had to go live in the home of strangers. My Mother also spent some time in the local children's home because her Mother could not afford to provide for the family needs for a season. Times were hard emotionally and financially for the whole family.

My parents were determined to keep our family together at all costs. They both knew they wanted to have a stable home for their child, especially because they knew the heartache of a broken one. Life was not always easy, but we learned through the adversity we faced in those days, due to limited income and situations we encountered along the paths of life each day.

I began to hear so many stories of folks going through adverse and painful experiences, and God seemed to send me those who opened up and shared their pain and sorrow. I would meet them as they came into my workplace or as someone began a conversation in the grocery store. I knew they all were divine appointments sent by God. My friends tell me all the time they believe I have a sign on my forehead that reads, "Tell me your entire life story. My friend, Debbie, tells me I need to learn to be "less approachable!"

Sometimes God asks us to step into the Jordan as an act of faith before He reveals any more instructions. I believe that has happened to me on my journey. I wanted to have it all spelled out before I began, but I found that God wanted me to step out and trust Him, and then He would show me the next step.

One particular Sunday, I packed up my things and went to our church prepared for a getaway afterwards to write. We were having a farewell party for one of the couples who had been a part of us for years because they were moving to Texas to be closer to their family. Many had brought goodies, and we were just having a good ole time of fellowship, nibbling as we talked.

As class began, Steve, our teacher, read from **Jeremiah 30:2 (NAS).** **"Thus says the Lord, the God of Israel: 'Write all the words that I have spoken to you in a book. ' "** Man, could God have made it any clearer than that to me? I wanted to just get up and shout! At this time I hadn't told the class that I was going to write a book, only a few who had been praying for me. I am wise enough to know I need people interceding for me in order to accomplish this task.

I had called for reservations in a quaint little spot on the mountain where my husband and I had visited many times before. When the guy at the facility asked me what kind of room I wanted, I said, "Just the cheapest one." He explained that if I wanted a room with a view, he could upgrade me. I said, "No, I will just take the cheaper one."

Upon entering the room, I could have been blown over with a feather. As I looked through the sliding glass doors, I could see the beautiful lake with the snow falling ever so gently, forming a thin sheet of ice on the water. The room featured a balcony with a wrought iron table and chairs which, if the weather cooperated, would be a great place to look out over the beautiful snow-covered grounds while I wrote.

Then I remembered that I had forgotten to bring my favorite glass coffee mug. I enjoy drinking out of glass mugs rather than the Styrofoam ones, which are usually provided in most hotels. Now is that asking too much? I want you to know that there beside the coffee pot were two glass coffee mugs. What a delight! You can tell me that all of this wasn't from God, but I won't believe it. **"Delight yourself in the LORD, and He will give you the desires of your heart" Psalm 37:4 (NIV)** states. Thank you, Father. You are faithful even in the little things that bring us pleasure when we delight in You.

One night before this get away, some friends and I went to hear Ruth Graham speak for a Christian counseling dinner. As Ruth shared about one of her heartaches, a dear friend, Carol, who was seated beside me, leaned over and said, "You should write a book." You see, God just kept speaking to me through people, His Word, and circumstances.

In many ways life has not been easy for our family. The story I am about to tell is my journey through many days of doubting, pain, tears, and struggle. My hope is it will not just be a story, but a help to you as you walk through your own valley experience.

A couple of years ago, I was listening to my favorite Christian radio station expounding on the goodness of God. A soft spoken lady said, "He was good because He gave her a child who was graduating from college with high honors." Then a man came on to say, "God was good because he had gotten a huge promotion." Another young voice explained God's goodness because she had been chosen for the cheerleading team. As I listened, I began to wonder if these same folks would give testimony of God's goodness even if their child had not graduated, or at least not with such high honors, or the man had lost his job instead of getting his promotion, or the young lady had not been chosen to cheer. What if their child had chosen to step into the world of addiction or their husband had developed some debilitating disease. Would God have still been good?

We tend to base God's goodness on the good things we receive from Him. Do you truly believe God is good all the time, even when you face fiery trials? Or when you begin to lose your health or when your finances take a dive? Or when you lose a loved one who is most precious to you? Or as in our case, your son turns to drugs and ends up in jail and then on to prison?

In my childhood days my Mother suffered with Manic Depression, now commonly referred to as Bi-Polar Disorder. In the sixties and seventies, not a lot was known about how to treat the disease. The stigma of mental illness is very unfair. If you have a physical disability you are usually shown empathy from others, but if you have a mental illness it is often times felt you could just get over it. That is not the case. She suffered many days of debilitating lows when she could not even take care of her personal needs. I have never known that depth of despair and can't even imagine her pain and sense of isolation. Not understanding the disease was tough on both she and her family.

It was not until after my marriage that my Dad was introduced to a Christian psychiatrist, a man we felt was sent by God to help my Mother. He prescribed Lithium, and it proved to be her miracle drug. She leveled out to some degree where the highs were not so high, nor the lows too low. Since taking this medication, Mother has done well and has felt so much better. I believe that even back during those childhood uncertainties; God was strengthening me and preparing me for the life to follow.

Following our marriage in 1970, we moved to Massachusetts for a year while Jimmy served in the Army. We busied ourselves with our new marriage relationship and our careers, but our relationship with God was not a priority. We visited some churches but were not very faithful. I began to feel myself drift away from the Godly principals I had been taught in my early years.

When we visited my Dad's church after our return home, God stirred my heart, and I could hardly wait for the message to end, so I could get down the aisle to rededicate my life to the Lord. That is where I began to be very involved in doing all I could to serve the Lord in whatever capacity I could. I never thought about seeking His face to know His perfect will for my life; I just plowed ahead with my own agenda. I thought the busier I was, the more it pleased the Father. After all I was doing His work wasn't I?

I had often heard the scripture in **1 Corinthians 3:11-15 (AMP), "For no other foundation can anyone lay than that which is [already] laid, which is Jesus Christ, the Messiah, the Anointed One. But if anyone builds on this Foundation whether it be with gold, silver, precious stones, wood, hay, straw. The work of each [one] will become (plainly, openly) known—shown for what it is; for the day (of Christ) will disclose and declare it because it will be revealed with fire, and the fire will test and critically appraise the character and worth of the work each person has done."** I believe those works I was doing at the time will definitely be burned up. I was busy doing things for God. I didn't realize His main objective was to draw me to Himself for fellowship and relationship.

In **Luke 10:38-42 (NKJV)** the story is told of Martha and Mary who were sisters:

"Now it happened as they went that He entered a certain village; and a certain woman named Martha welcomed Him into her house. And she had a sister called Mary, who also sat at Jesus' feet and heard His word. But Martha was distracted with much serving, and she approached Him and said, 'Lord, do You not care that my sister has left me to serve alone? Therefore tell her to help me.' And Jesus answered and said to her, 'Martha, Martha, you are worried and troubled about many things. But one thing is needed, and Mary has chosen that good part, which will not be taken away from her.' "

Boy was I a Martha. I was busy all the time with household duties, work, tending to children, and doing my good works at church. I didn't have time to sit at Jesus' feet as Mary did. After all, how was all the work going to be accomplished if I sat down? But the passage says, Mary chose the better place.

I had learned as a child that there was no down time. If I sat down, I had to either be writing a note to my grandparents, ironing, or mending. You didn't just sit idly. I've always loved to read, so times were spent reading, but I certainly didn't read the Word at length. Maybe a passage or two in my time alone with Him before the day started. As I look back now, I know I missed the mark terribly.

All that has changed and you can't keep me out of His Word now. If you gave me one thing to retrieve out of a burning house I would choose my big Parallel Bible which has come to mean so much to me. It has dates and notes all over it that really show my walk with the Lord and how He has spoken to me over the years. The Word has become alive to me, and I cherish the moments God has spoken to me through it. He is so faithful, and I love Him more each day.

I picked up a book a few years ago by Hannah Hurnard, Hinds' Feet on High Places. It is an allegory of Much Afraid's journey through life's struggles with the Shepherd. Much Afraid is invited by the Shepherd to follow Him to the High Places. She is too afraid at first to come out of her cottage, but He keeps wooing her. Finally, she has the courage to step out, but she believes she will be going straight to the High Place and is disappointed to find out it may take a while. Not only that, but her traveling companions were named Sorrow and Suffering. Her choice for companions would have been Joy and Peace.

She believes that the Shepherd is having her follow the path too long and it is too steep to climb. She thinks He has forgotten His promises to her. The Shepherd is in the process of turning her weaknesses into strengths and her fears into faith. She has to learn to trust Him. He leads her through danger and tribulation and tells her not to fear because He is with her. She is learning when the storms come up, she still can have peace. All she has to do is call on Him, and He will be right by her side. She has to learn to walk by faith, not by sight.

She learns that only one thing really matters--to do the will of the One she follows no matter what it involves or what the cost is. As she comes to the end of her journey and reaches the high places, her companions' names then change to Joy and Peace. But she can't stay on the High Place because as she looks back down in the valley she sees those who are still bound in fear. She decides to go back down to tell them they can be free if they choose to follow the Shepherd.

You see, Much Afraid thought the journey would be without trouble, but she found that God changed her heart *because* of the trials and troubles she learned to walk through. It wasn't an easy journey, but a necessary one, if she were to mature in Him.[1]

Sometimes that is what we think, that the journey will be and should be an easy one free of trials and afflictions. However it is in the valleys we grow. Are you willing to step out in faith and follow the Shepherd no matter where it takes you? You'll have to die to the flesh and trust Him.

I have looked upon my life as a journey also. Many times I have been too afraid to step out in faith. Many times I made the wrong choices and failed. Many times I just plain didn't trust the Shepherd. But as I've followed and stayed close to Him, I have learned to hear His voice and to be more obedient to His call.

I have also discovered that once I made it to the high place with Him I could not look back down in the valley and see the struggles of others without being touched by a desire to walk alongside them to offer hope and encouragement.

> *Prayer: Lord, continue to teach me to be obedient to Your call and direction for my life. You know I love you with all my heart and soul, so I desire to be so willing to follow You that I do it immediately without wrestling with You or second guessing, Amen.*

CHAPTER THREE

When God Calls, He Provides

"And my God will liberally supply (fill to the full) your every need according to His riches in glory in Christ Jesus." Philippians 4:19, (AMP).

In 1990 a missionary visited Calvary Baptist Church in Winston-Salem, North Carolina where Jimmy and I are members. This missionary called for short term missionaries to accept the call of God to come to Kenya to help spread the Gospel. They planned to have a crusade in July of that year and needed many volunteers to come to join in with them. He was a career missionary and had come to the states to ask those of us who felt led to join him in this endeavor.

As I sat in the balcony, I felt the prompting of the Holy Spirit to answer the call. My heart began to race, and I began to give God all the excuses I could find not to go down to the altar. After all, I had a young family and worked fulltime to help provide for the needs of the family. I literally had to hold on to the rail in front of me to keep from stepping into the aisle. I continued to be under such conviction that I finally said, "Okay Lord, I will go down, but I still don't see how in the world I can do it." The only way I got complete peace was to go down the aisle. It was a long way down to the front from the balcony, but I made it before the invitation closed.

I decided I would go to the first planning meeting and see what they had to say. We had a time of prayer together during the meeting, and I continued to feel the strong call of the Lord.

The financial information was given, and it was explained that the church would pay half our cost. That was a real plus. On my way home I began to practice what I would say to my husband who would not be so thrilled with my news.

As Jimmy and I discussed the trip upon my return it was clear he didn't want me to go. We had never been separated for even one day and this trip would be for eighteen days. He would have to be responsible for the home front, and I believe it was just a combination of concerns. He finally told me I could not go. I just told the Father that if he wanted me to go, He would have to speak to my husband.

I went down the hall to prepare for bed and work the next day and Jimmy came in no more than ten minutes later to apologize. He expressed that if God had called me then he couldn't go against that. Wow! Was that ever a faith builder for me in answer to prayer!

Two more details would have to come together before I could go. Those included the time off from work and an available spot for me on the team of thirty. Needless to say, I went straight to my boss on Monday when I arrived at work and approached him with the idea of being off eighteen days to go on a mission trip. Before I left work that day, I had his approval.

My parents were in town and came by to see me that afternoon, so I was able to share with them the call I had received and how God was working it out. They actually took my $100 deposit to the church for me, so I could get my name on the list as soon as possible.

I knew my Dad had always wanted to go to Africa as a missionary in his early years, but because of health issues at the time, the door was closed. He was so excited to know that I would be going to literally fulfill his dream.

I decided I needed to get another job on the weekends to help finance the trip, so I went to work at the nearby nursing home doing 12-hour shifts in addition to my fulltime job during the week. After two weekends of this I prayed, "Lord, I am so tired I just don't believe I can do this anymore". It was almost like I heard Him speak in an audible voice, "I didn't ask you to, did I?" He did speak to my spirit, and it was the last extra work I did.

My daughter, Melissa, a friend, and I went to the Christmas cantata at our church and out to eat together afterwards. I was so excited sharing with them about my call to go to Kenya. As we left the restaurant, my friend gave me a check for $100 explaining how she wanted to be a part of the trip. Another friend gave me $40, and my parents mailed me a check for $100. Jimmy came home one day in January to tell me he had received a 10% raise due to the revamping of his job description. Wow! It was quite unexpected by us, but not by God. He had called me to go, and I was learning that when He calls, He provides.

The next week Jimmy called me to say that the ladies he worked with wanted me to come by after work. They surprised me with a lovely card which had $100 in it for my trip. They had taken up a collection among themselves, and it was such a blessing.

In the meantime, I talked to my Mother about the possibility of their church sending my Dad on the trip with us. She spoke to the chairman of the deacon board, and he presented the idea to the board. They decided to help finance the mission trip for my Dad so that he could go with us.

We decided to surprise him with the announcement at one of their Wednesday night services. Jimmy and I drove down and presented my Dad with the news that he would be going to Kenya with me. We were all so overcome with emotion. My Dad was in absolute shock as we left the church. He was speechless for a long time because he was just overwhelmed.

My support for the trip came in first from one source and then from another as people handed me checks or cash stating they wanted to be a part of what God was doing. God had shown us His power to accomplish what He desired me to do. It had been an awesome experience just in the preparation. I couldn't wait to see what He has in store for us on this journey.

The night before we were to leave, we invited some friends, who were definite prayer warriors, over for prayer time. I felt covered with that special time we had with the Lord. I knew the value of intercessors that would be in constant prayer for our group as we traveled and served.

The day had arrived, and I realized that it was going to be hard to say farewell to my family and friends. I had never done much flying either, so this was going to be a fairly new experience. I asked Jimmy if I could back out. He told me not to start that because more than likely he was having second thoughts also.

I found traveling to be the hardest part of the trip. We stopped in London and were able to do a short tour of the area before we headed on. It was fun seeing Big Ben and Buckingham Palace and St. Paul's Cathedral where Princess Di and Prince Charles were married, but I was anxious to proceed with the journey.

We met with a large group from all over the US who would be traveling with us from London on Kenya Air. We filled up that plane for the most part. We had a great time singing and praising the Father in anticipation of the call He had on all our lives. The trip was long and tiring and I was more than ready to put my feet on solid ground again. To be able to stretch out on a real bed would be awesome!

We were flying amongst the white fluffy clouds, which looked like cotton. It looked as if you could just float on them. They appeared as far as the eye could see. It was a gorgeous sight to someone who had not flown much.

I turned to **Psalm 118:24 (NIV), "This is the day that the Lord hath made. We will rejoice and be glad in it."** In verse 25 it says, **"O Lord, grant us success."** Oh yes, that was my prayer for the trip.

We are getting close to Kenya now. The pilot tells us we are passing over Nairobi the capital of Kenya. Now we see Mount Kilimanjaro in the distance. I am getting so excited. As we step off the plane, we hear the singing of the missionaries as they welcome us.

The airport facilities are very primitive. Someone points out a monkey in the tree. We are definitely in Africa! We have our luggage, now and the nationals pile up their vans with our luggage, and off we go to the orientation meeting where the details of where we will stay and what we will be doing will be presented.

Another short-term missions group was here for two weeks before we arrived, and we were told that 21,000 were saved, and several churches were started in their area.

We will be going into a little town on the east coast bordered by the Indian Ocean. We are so pumped up to go and begin the work in the villages that it is hard to wait.

I am already feeling like we have been gone from home for three weeks instead of only three days. We are all very tired and strongly encouraged not to go to bed, so we can get acclimated to the time difference of seven hours. We have not seen a bed since we left home, and a shower would sure be in order now. We still are not at our hotel. We have a little more traveling to do this evening before we can get settled in.

We traveled a very long way on a dirt road to get to our hotel. I told my Dad, "If someone had told me I would be going down the road doing about 90 mph in Africa one day, I would have told them they were crazy!"

I admit I had become a little discouraged and tired, wondering if this was where I should be. God took me to **Psalm 91:15 (KJV), "He shall call upon me, and I will answer him: I will be with him in trouble; I will deliver him and honor him."** Lord, give me strength to endure.

After a good night's sleep under mosquito nets enveloping our beds, just like you see in the movies, we went to breakfast. Their scrambled eggs looked very interesting, and the croissants certainly weren't made by Sara Lee! I finally found something to eat, and then we were off for the hotel we would stay for the next two weeks.

We were taken across the river in a ferry boat, and began to meet some of the nationals as we waited to cross. We saw many grass huts on our way to our destination. The people were impoverished immediately beyond the big cities.

Our room is very simple but nice. There is a shower, but I discover there is only cold water to bathe with. Everything is very open here, including the dining area. It's like eating outside. At dinner they serve salad, raw vegetables, bread, meat, baked fish, and potatoes. Not bad. The coffee is so strong I believe your spoon could stand up all by itself. We learned to mix half coffee and half water.

The next morning, the focus of my quiet time is how God uses people for His purposes. That is my desire, that He use me today and everyday anyway he sees fit. As I turn in His Word I read from **Luke 18:29-30 (NIV), "I tell you the truth Jesus said to them, no one who has left home or wife or brothers or parents or children for the sake of the kingdom of God will fail to receive many times as much in this age and, in the age to come, eternal life."** Thank you Lord for that Word this morning as I am struggling being away from my family. Help me to love those I meet today with the love of Christ.

When we arrived at the village where we would minister this morning, we met our interpreter, Julius, and Joseph, the pastor of the church. These were young men. Julius was a pastor's son and seemed strong in his walk. Joseph said he went to church a long time without accepting Christ into his heart but finally did about three years before.

As we went into the villages, Joseph had to ask permission from the elder in that village to see if we could come in and share the gospel with them. We were never once refused entrance into anyone's home. The nationals were very hospitable.

In this first village, the elder was very sick and could not go to the church. We were asked to pray for this man who had swollen and sore legs. We prayed for him, and he thanked us many times for coming.

At our next stop six people came to know the Lord after a member of our team shared with them. I was blown away by the readiness of the people to receive. God had certainly gone before us. It took us several times to realize that they were ready. We felt we needed to go into more detail and share more with them before they could receive Him, but it became crystal clear that when the interpreter told us they were ready to pray to ask Jesus into their hearts, they truly were.

As soon as we went into each village the women would bring stools made from tree stumps or tin pails for us to sit on. They were unbelievably hospitable.

We had to learn to speak through an interpreter which was hard to get used to, but we eventually learned to slow down and give them time to interpret for the people.

There were animals everywhere, chickens, a few cows, goats, donkeys, and dogs. They were looking very skinny and malnourished. These animals even walked into the straw huts. I stuck my head in to speak to one of the people one day, and a chicken flew up at me and scared me to death!

We attempted to learn some simple Swahili words and say them. The interpreters and the people would laugh at us. As we walked down the trail past the villages, we would holler out to them, "Good afternoon," in Swahili. . I guess Swahili with a southern twang does sound pretty funny!

The people are pitiful. Most of them wear clothing but some women go bare-breasted, and they nursed their babies out in the open. Their method for using the bathroom was much the same. They just squatted down most anywhere, especially if a choo was not available to them. A choo was a big hole in the ground that you just squatted down over. I found out very quickly why we were told to carry toilet tissue and hand sanitizer with us.

Why there was no more sickness and disease then there appeared to be was beyond me. Their living conditions were so unsanitary. As I stated earlier, the chickens ran wild, even into their homes, with droppings left everywhere. Flies were abundant.

The women carried large buckets of water, vegetables, and more on their heads, just like you see in the National Geographic. The men walk ahead of them and make the decisions for them. We even had some women who wanted to pray to receive Christ who couldn't because their husbands would not allow them to. I always prayed that they made the decisions for themselves within their own hearts.

The church where we were worshipping actually built the facility themselves. Most of the equipment was donated by the International Mission Board of the Southern Baptist Convention. The building was made with the mud and cement over top of that. There are about ten benches made from split logs. The children mostly sat on the floor.

Their worship and singing time was amazing. Even though we could not understand the words, the spirit of the songs and their voices come through loud and strong. The ladies in particular loved to sing. They had a choir of adults and a choir of children.

We were informed today that we would be teaching at the church every afternoon. That meant we would be up in front of the whole church. Whew! I certainly would be out of my comfort zone. God was leading me into all kinds of things I had never done before, so I knew He'd provide the words for me to share tomorrow as I attempt to teach about prayer.

The first home we came to was one we revisited because the elder and his wife were gone to a burial, so we came back to share with them. We were informed that when someone died and they had a burial, everyone in the village attended the service. If they did not they were thought to have had something to do with the person's death and were under suspicion.

Back to the family, the elder was very attentive as we shared and asked some questions. Then he and his wife and two children prayed to receive Christ. We left him reading the Gospel of John in Swahili. The people were more open to receiving the good news here than back at home. We asked questions to make sure they understood, and they responded that they did, so we accepted by faith that they fully comprehended what they were doing.

They all seemed to be so happy! With all the poverty, sickness, and lack of material wealth, they still seemed content and happy with their situation. The children often had only one ball to play with in their home, or they played with old bike tires, metal rings, or homemade slingshots. They made balls out of wadded up plastic bags wrapped into a round ball and held together with the basket straw. They found whatever they could to entertain themselves. The children ran and played, helped with chores, and took care of their brothers and sisters. They smiled at us as they played their games.

I was reminded of home and all the things American children think they must have to be happy, and it saddened me. We've placed our values on all the wrong things, thus we are still unfulfilled. I would have loved for my children to have been with me to witness this fact.

The people were stress free it appeared, unlike us Americans. Time was not important. The announced time for church to begin at 4:45, but it was roughly 5:15 before everyone straggled in and the service started.

Joseph and Julius, the pastor of the church and our interpreter, brought their lunches to the church to join us. They had two fish in a bowl of milky liquid and a pan of ugali, which would be comparable to our cornbread. They pulled away the bread with their fingers and worked with it in their hands to make a ball of dough. Then they dipped it in the fish liquid and ate it. It was not very appetizing to us, needless to say. We were happy with our square meals, as my son-in-law says, that we had brought from home. Nabs!

They got coconuts and broke them open for us to enjoy the coconut milk and some of its meat. We also had a mango which was very tasty and sweet. Both were very plentiful that time of year. We saw the children eating mangos everywhere we went.

I asked if there were many snakes in the area. The answer was yes, but the snakes didn't come around the area very often. They have a two-headed snake there which was very poisonous.

As we were going down the path, Julius said a snake had just been across the path because we saw its imprint in the dirt. Ugh! I told him to pray really hard for us not to see one. I don't like snakes.

In one home, I sat on one of the beds. It was fairly comfortable. They are just a bed frame with braided rope pulled from side to side to hold you up and sometimes they use a mat on it to sleep.

We saw a woman grinding corn for meal. She put it in a flat basket with small open holes and then sifted it. The chickens liked eating the part that was sifted out through the open holes and then landed on the ground. The rest was saved for bread and porridge, cooked much like our cream of wheat.

We were able to go into a Muslim village and share with them. The men were away, and the women were a little hesitant to invite us in but finally did. We shared about the love of Christ as He died on the cross for us and our need to repent of our sins and to invite Him into our hearts. They said they understood our message, but they couldn't have two gods. We explained that there is only one true God, but they said it would be impossible for them to receive Him without the permission of their husbands. How sad! They did accept our booklets of the Gospel of John and said that they would share them with their husbands.

The fatigue set in one morning and the devil was working also because I'm feeling overwhelmed with homesickness. When we got to the church they asked me to pray, and I almost didn't make it as I started crying. It was very hard to make it through the prayer. I was certainly not feeling the desire to go tell others of Jesus' love because I was feeling very much alone, but as we moved on throughout the day I prayed for God's strength and to get my mind set on the task ahead, and He did.

Don't get me wrong, sharing here with these people was very exciting and fulfilling, but I was missing my family. God brought me to **Philippians 4:13 (NAS), "I can do all things through Christ who strengthens me".** I claimed that as God's promise to me.

God helped us and used us even through our weariness and depression. It was amazing. The first home we visited, the entire household accepted the Lord. There was an elder and several younger men there. The elder said that because of his position in the family he could not accept. He said his culture required him to marry his dead brother's wives. He believed that the Bible taught against that so he could not receive Christ. We talked, and God showed me a scripture about receiving Christ in whatever state we are in. In other words, no matter what position we are in, if we seek His forgiveness and invite Him in, He will accept us into His family

His wife, who was already a believer, begged him to receive God's forgiveness for his sin and accept Him into his heart. After she talked to him, he came running up to us with his stool and sat right down in front of us and said he was ready! He thanked us many times for coming to share with him.

As we left that home, we came upon a group of men and realized that they had been drinking. We shared some with them but told them that in the condition they were in we would like for them to come to church on Sunday. One of the men was actually Joseph's father. One of them lived in the next home we went to visit, and his wife prayed to receive Christ.

I was able to call home and talk to everyone. Our son, Robbie, was celebrating his birthday so I had waited to call on that special day. I felt bad for not being there. It was good to talk to my family. I thought it might make me more homesick, but I actually felt much better afterwards. Guess I never realized how much the three words, "I love you", can mean after not hearing them for a while.

We had taken candy for the children and as I brought it out I was almost mobbed. They rarely received any sweets, so this was a very special treat for them. There were about 75 kids that attended Sunday school. We had a great time together. I tried to teach them "Jesus loves me", so they could sing it for their parents later, but it was difficult.

As we gathered for worship, I noticed many of them did not have Bibles, and song books were very scarce. We had some Bibles at the hotel in translated into Swahili. We tried to take some with us everywhere we went, so we could give them out.

God provided us with some much needed rest, and most of us headed out for our safari experience for an overnight stay where you could hear the animals. The rooms were screened in, so we could go to sleep by the sounds of the night. We traveled to get there on washboard roads and began to wonder if we had made a mistake to come. Our minds changed as we entered the park and saw gazelles, elephants, zebras, secretary birds, and giraffes. What a sight! We rode in open vans in order to stand up and see the animals as they came into view.

As we broke for lunch, we were entertained by the baboons. The waiters had to keep shooing them away from our table and warned us not to leave with a banana visible in our hands because the baboons might charge us. At times the waiter had to use a slingshot to get the baboons to move away from the dining area.

We went out to the overlook after lunch. There was a manmade water hole below us, and the animal kingdom took turns coming for a drink. The monkeys and baboons blanketed the rocks and hills.

The view was beyond description. Using my binoculars, I could look out and see hundreds of elephants approaching the water hole. The different species of animals seemed to take turns. As one group finished the next ones came to get water and sometimes to wash.

A group of zebras came up very cautiously to get water. Their apparent leader kept looking around to make sure no lions were roaming about. One of the zebras had a very bad cut on his side where he had been attacked. They appeared to be as interested in looking at us as we were at them.

As I sat and looked out over the range, I wished once again that my family were here to enjoy this with me. It was such a spectacular sight; one I never dreamed I would be a part of. Thank you, Father, for this opportunity to see the majesty of your creation. How I wonder what Adam might have felt as he first saw all the animals and had the task of naming them!

We observed the elephants coming out of the woods from long distances for water. I pondered how God created the animals with the instinct of fear for their own protection and how He gave each one of them the ability to protect themselves in one way or another by the way He created them.

We were told that the gazelles have one male in their group who stays with several females for 60-70 days and mates with them and guards them. Then they run him out, and another male is invited in the group, and the first male goes out by himself for 60-70 days to rest and eat. Then it goes and finds a new group of females to join. Isn't that interesting?

We made our way back to the hotel to begin preparations for our second week of ministry. We were divided into different groups for the upcoming week in order to visit different villages. My group went into the home of a lady whose neck glands were very swollen. It was believed that she had some type of cancer. I asked if she had been to the doctor, and she said, "No." She visited the witch doctor. Her name was Tabu. Her Mother was there with her to cook and take care of her daughter. Tabu really touched my heart. She could not swallow very well and was only able to eat porridge. Her Mother asked us to pray for her. I shared the Gospel, and she and her Mother prayed to receive Christ. Afterwards I prayed with them and explained to them that now they had access directly to God through prayer now, and they didn't have to wait for someone else to pray for them.

This village area was a little more affluent than the one from the previous week. We saw lots of cattle and more goats here. The people seemed to be dressed a little better also. The pastor's home had some fencing and a gazebo with a table and chairs under it. They had planted some flowers planted around their walkway, which was marked off and neatly landscaped.

We revisited the home where Tabu lived and found her feeling very poorly. We left some medicine for her pain and promised to visit again the next day.

I called home again. Everybody sounded good. It was countdown to being homeward bound now. Jimmy encouraged me to enjoy my time now because he would not let me go anymore. Ha. I believe he was missing me a little.

As we were sharing in a village, some women came up with bunches of bananas in a basket on their heads. It was amazing to see what they could balance on their heads, bundles of firewood, bottles of milk, and whole jugs of water. Whew! I could envision me trying to carry all that weight on my head. I have too many headaches as it is.

There were no washers and dryers here, so we hand washed everything. The hotel washed the towels and laid them out on the grass to dry. They were stiff as boards and changed only every two to three days. Man, that wouldn't fly in American would it?

Simon, one of our interpreters, brought me a gift today. He had made both the basket and the necklace. It was very special to me. The only thing I have to give them is soap which they seem pleased to receive. We will also leave most of our clothes to be distributed by the missionaries.

As we reunited to share our experiences, we had a very emotional time. One young man even felt the call to go home and prepare to return to be a career missionary. Our missionaries had been fantastic and really had worked these last two weeks or more to provide us places to go and interpreters to assist us.

The missionaries warned us in the beginning that we would probably leave part of our hearts here in Africa, and they were right. I was ready to go home, but with mixed emotions. We had witnessed God working in such a mighty way. Now I know what Jesus meant in the passage in **Luke 10:2 (KJV), "Therefore said he unto them. The harvest truly is great, but the laborers are few; therefore pray the Lord of the harvest to send out laborers into His harvest."**

On our last day there, we met in the church, and it was filled to overflow. The children sat all over the floor, and we had a time of worship that I knew it was pleasing to the Father. The nationals songs and voices will forever ring in my ears and heart.

I told them as I spoke for the last time that they had taught me far more than I had taught them. It was a trip that I would never forget. When we arrived in London, my Dad and I along with many others from the trip went to the nearest McDonald's. I can't even tell you what I paid in pounds, but it was the best meal I had had in two weeks.

We arrived home safely with much to share with anyone who would listen. I knew the faces of the people would remain permanently etched in my minds. I took many photographs, and I plan on reviewing them often. I wouldn't take anything for the experiences we had. I believe God taught me His provision at this time in preparation for the journey I was about to embark on. My mind was often drawn back to this lesson as He walked with me in the years to come.

Prayer: I thank You God for the opportunity to go as Your ambassador to a people so needy and hungry for the Word. Thank you for the decisions made there in that country. Most of all, thank You for the lessons You taught me through the difficulties I encountered. Thank You for showing me that when You call, You provide, Amen.

CHAPTER FOUR

There is Hope in Our Future

"This is what the LORD said, A voice is heard in Ramah, mourning and great weeping, Rachel weeping for her children, and refusing to be comforted, because her children, are no more. This is what the LORD says: 'Restrain your voice from weeping and your eyes from tears; for your work shall be rewarded.' They shall return from the land of the enemy. So there is hope for your future,' your children will return to their own land.'" Jeremiah 31:15-17, (NIV).

After my mission trip to Kenya in 1990, life took a sharp turn for our family as we marched and sometimes dragged through the trials and struggles that would come our way. The enemy seemed to be hard at work in our family. He brought temptations into my life that I thought I was strong enough to resist. After all, I was working for God, wasn't I?

I was hard at work in the church. Busy, busy, busy. I found out that in my weakness, I needed God more and more. Or was this a test from the Lord? If so I failed it miserably. I had succumbed to things I swore I would never do. Has that ever occurred with you? God revealed my weakness and my pride where I thought I was above yielding to sin, breaking my spirit down in total repentance and submission to Him.

Did you realize God tests us? The Word says He doesn't tempt us, but He does test us. A test is defined as something that manifests a person's real character. We have many examples of men tested by God: Moses, Abraham, Noah, Jonah, David, Job, Daniel, and the list continues.

King Darius was thinking of placing Daniel as ruler over his whole realm. The governors and satraps set out to bring some charge against Daniel but could find none. Knowing that Daniel prayed to his God faithfully, they made a decree that anyone seen petitioning their god instead of the king for 30 days would be thrown into the lion's den. Daniel passed the test when he bowed down three times that day with his window open for all to witness just as he always did. He worshipped the One and Only true God. He was not ashamed or afraid of the king's decree. His actions brought glory to the Father as God showed His power to deliver him from the lion's den unharmed.

God allowed Satan to test Job to demonstrate that Job would continue to serve Him in His loss. His family, land, stock, houses, and health were taken from him. Satan had gone before God to proclaim that the reason Job served Him was because he had a hedge of protection around him. Satan believed with the hedge removed and his possessions taken from him, Job would curse God. Job was a man who feared God and shunned evil. So God allowed the testing of Job, and even though there were moments he questioned and doubted, Job remained faithful, and God blessed him in his latter years more than his earlier years. I have often thought how I would like to be known to God as Job was. God so trusted Job's response to the test that he even said to Satan, "Have you considered my servant, Job?" Wow!

Sometimes the test comes at God's call for an assignment or special task He wants us to accomplish in His name. That was the test Jonah was given and failed. He even tried to run from the presence of the Lord.

"Where can I go from Your Spirit? Or where can I flee from Your presence? If I ascend into the heavens, you are there; if I make my bed in hell, behold, you are there. If I take the wings of the morning, and dwell in the uttermost parts of the sea, even there Your hand shall hold me," states **Psalm 139:7-10 (AMP)**.

I used to wonder why God didn't just let Jonah stay in the belly of the great fish since he did not want to obey Him, but I am so grateful that He didn't leave me there. God used me in spite of my disobedience. What an awesome God we serve! He is a God of second, third, and even more chances. We may have to suffer the consequences of our bad choices, but

He will use us to accomplish His purposes as we surrender to Him in total repentance and obedience.

Abram's test was a test of faith. **Genesis 12:1-3 (NKJV) says, "Now the Lord had said to Abram: Get out of your country, from your kindred and from your father's house, to a land that I will show you. I will make you a great nation; I will bless you and make your name great; and you shall be a blessing. I will bless those who bless you, and I will curse him who curses you; and in you all the families of the earth shall be blessed."**

Verse 4 says, **"So Abram departed as the Lord had spoken to him....And he was 75 years old."**

I am impressed not only that he stepped out in faith and obedience, but he was 75 years old when he did it! At that age most of us have sunk our roots down deep and have made our plans for the rest of our days. Many think God is through giving assignments at that age. They feel they have worked all their lives and deserve to do as they please.

I remember going on the mission trip to Africa and being amazed at the ones over 70 who accompanied us, including my own Dad. Physically, it was hard to get adjusted and do all the walking and be out in the villages for hours, but I heard none of them complaining. They knew they were being obedient to the call of God on their lives, and He would bless them because of it.

David's test was keeping the law given by God to Moses. He failed not only the commandment which spoke of not committing adultery, but also the one which instructed us not to covet your neighbor's house nor your neighbor's wife.

His disobedience led him deeper and deeper into sin, even to the act of murder. He tried to cover up his sin, just as we do sometimes, thinking no one would know. So God sent Nathan to confront him with his sin. How did David respond?

In Psalm 51 we have David's prayer of repentance and his restoration with his Lord. That restoration did not occur until David was willing to cry out to God for mercy. I imagine David was lying face down before God in agony because of his sin.

Ever been there? Just flippantly saying I am sorry doesn't do it; we must be utterly sorrowful for our sin and then turn and walk in the opposite direction, which truly defines repentance. This is the only way we can be cleansed and used by the Lord in the future. Aren't we grateful for His grace which allows us to be restored to Him?

We all fail at points in our lives. We may fail just as some of these men did. The reason we aren't left in the belly of the great fish or put on a shelf or even taken out of this life is because God hears our cry and forgives our trespasses.

Jonah might not have wanted to go to Nineveh, but he went in obedience given the second chance because he responded positively to the discipline of God. The Lord can certainly take us to the woodshed if we are disobedient. I've been there many times but don't want to return.

We were facing other tests which involved our son at this time. Around age seven, he was diagnosed with learning disabilities and attention deficit disorder. He was doing poorly in school and with his social skills. We began taking him to tutors even at that early age. He seemed to be doing much better with his studies but continued to have problems socially.

Robbie began to hang around with the wrong crowd and was showing more and more signs of rebellion. We took him to a counselor at church who told us after meeting with him that he was " just a normal little boy" which relieved my mind for the moment, but we were still concerned about the behaviors we were observing. Something about a Mother's intuition told me that what we were seeing was not normal. We did a lot of grounding in those days, seemingly to no avail.

Our son loved to play little league baseball and we loved to go to the games. He was a born athlete and we looked forward to years of watching him and cheering him on. His Dad had been a baseball star in High School and we hoped that Robbie would follow in those same footsteps.

I grieve over the loss of this time together as a family as I look out my kitchen window watching our young neighbor and his Dad practicing ball together. Seeing him in his baseball uniform brings to mind that little green baseball suit our son wore as he played for his team so many years ago. We have many pictures of him over the years playing, and I did have them on the walls until Rob asked me to take them down. I believe it is a very sad reminder to him of years lost also.

After our daughter, Melissa, graduated from High School, we decided to move away from the community and expose our son to new friends and surroundings. We thought a new location would solve all the issues, but we were soon to find that would not be the case.

We rarely seemed to have a moment's problem with our daughter, Melissa, and could not understand why things were so much of a problem with our son. He did well in the first weeks of school after we moved, but then he was introduced to marijuana in the ninth grade, and the heartaches worsened.

I got a call one day from the school principal that our son was in the office and had been giving some of his things away and telling people good-bye. He had told them he was going to kill himself. I left work immediately, jumped in my car, and drove to the school to pick him up. He seemed very lethargic, so much so that I barely made it to the car with him. I had already called the psychiatrist he was seeing at the time who instructed me to bring him straight to his office. After meeting with the doctor, he recommended that we put Robbie in the hospital for observation. He remained in this psychiatric facility for three weeks to receive counseling, peer group sessions, and daily meetings with the doctor. How much good this did I still wonder about.

I can still remember the tears that flowed down my cheeks as I turned to leave him in that place. He wanted to know why he couldn't go home, and I tried to explain that he was going to get some help for the problems he had had. I assured him we would be back to see him as soon as the medical personnel would allow us.

As I turned to leave, I caught a glimpse of his face, and he seemed so afraid and lost. I cried all the way home, but this would not be the last of my tears. I remembered the passage in **Psalm 30:5b (KJV), "Weeping may endure for a night, but joy cometh in the morning."** I wondered when my joy would return as I drove away with a crushed and heavy heart for our son.

The psychiatrist told us that Robbie might be Bi-Polar. He displayed a lot of the symptoms with bouts of depression, mood swings, up times, and down times. Sometimes the disease is passed down through the generations within a family, so it made sense to me. The doctor prescribed Lithium, and they began to give it to him but found that he was not swallowing the medicine. They started giving it to him in liquid form watching him swallow it. He seemed to be coping somewhat better, so we were encouraged.

We went to group sessions with other parents, and some of the situations were so sad. I still was not convinced that it was not just the drug use that had presented the symptoms but time would tell.

After what seemed like a very long time to us, we were finally told we could take him home. He was to take lithium twice a day, and I gave it to him and watched him take it. He went back to school and seemed to do well for a while.

He had some special classes to help with the learning disabilities, and we even tried Ritalin along the way to help him concentrate enough to get his school work done. Nothing seemed to help for very long.

In earlier years we took him to psychologists for counseling in attempts to find out what was going on with him and also for tutoring. We were grasping for any help we could get at this point, and it proved to be a very costly adventure.

We used all kinds of discipline, grounding, lack of phone privileges, no wheels, no TV, all the usual techniques that seem to work for so many folks and for our daughter, but none were successful. He had such a rebellious spirit and was drawn to the wrong crowd mainly because he was accepted by them when others rejected him.

At age seventeen he left home for a few days and stayed with some friends. I knew in my heart he must be involved with drugs at the time, but he was very good at hiding his use. I drove to places I thought he might be, called his regular friends, and talked to their parents but no one seemed to have seen him. I paced the floors many nights looking out the window, hoping for his car to turn into our driveway. I kept the phone nearby me hoping it would ring, and I would hear his voice.

I cried out to the Lord in my desperation to bring him home and protect him while he was gone. My heart was aching. I knew we made many mistakes in those days, but we did the best we knew how.

Our daughter, Melissa, had her wedding quickly approaching, so I was involved in planning that and trying to stay composed for her, yet at the same time so concerned about Robbie. I prayed and prayed that he would show up in time for the wedding because it was breaking Melissa's heart to think he might not be home in time to be in her wedding.

Finally, we did receive that call and three days before the wedding Robbie came home. We did a lot of talking and reminded him of the house rules again. We knew we couldn't keep going this route. We tried to get him help with the drugs, but I believe he was continuing to use despite our efforts to get him to stop.

Many times I talked to him about the music he was listening to. I took away some of the CD's he had and threw them away, but he would come home with more of them. I warned him about the influence the words that were being sung would have on him. He responded, "I just like the beat, I don't listen to the words."

It wasn't long after that that I received a newsletter from James Dobson which read as follows:

> "Specifically, my letter this month reflects some conversations I've been having with hurting parents who feel defeated and demoralized by problems with their kids. Most of these moms and dads are wonderfully devoted to

their families. Nothing has been withheld in their zeal to be good parents. Yet the harder they've tried and the greater their sacrifice, the more their kids seem to resent them. There are millions of good mothers and fathers in this pressure cooker today.

Adolescent rebellion hasn't always been so prevalent, of course. In previous centuries teens were capable of resisting authority but the culture didn't bait them to do it. Children were taught to respect their parents, and those who didn't were thought of as "bad kids". But today, anger is in the air.

Even youngsters from loving homes are often taught to defy their moms and dads by the television they watch, by the movies they see, and by what they hear other children say and do. And certainly, this spirit of rebellion is a centerpiece of today's rock music.

Consider, for example, how the music of the culture has changed in just five decades. I recalled in my book Life on the Edge that the most popular song in the United States in 1953 was sung by Eddie Fisher and was title "Oh! My Papa." Here's a portion of the lyrics:

"Oh, my papa, to me he was so wonderful
Oh, my papa, to me he was so good
No one could be so gentle and so lovable
Oh, my papa, he always understood
Gone are the days when he would take me on his knee
And with a smile he'd change my tears to Laughter
Oh, my papa, so funny and adorable
Always the clown, so funny in his way
Oh, my papa, to me he was so wonderful
Deep in my heart, I miss him so today
Oh, my papa, Oh, my papa"

That sentimental song accurately reflected the way many people felt about their fathers at that time in our history, Oh sure, there were conflicts and disagreements, but family was family. When it was all said and done, parents were

41

entitled to respect and loyalty, and they usually received it from their children.

By the time I had reached college things were starting to change. The subject of conflict between parents and teenagers began to appear as a common theme in artistic creations.

Some early rock 'n' roll lyrics mixed rebellious messages with humor, such as a number-one hit from 1958 called "Yakety Yak (Don't Talk Back)." But what began as musical humor turned decidedly bitter in the late '60's. Everyone in those days was talking about the "generation gap" that had erupted between young people and their parents. Teenagers and college students vowed they'd never again trust anyone over 30, and their anger toward parents began to percolate. The Doors released a song in 1968 entitled "The End," in which Jim Morrison fantasized about killing his father. It concluded with gunshots followed by horrible grunts and groans.

In 1984, Twisted Sister released "We're Not Gonna Take it," which referred to a father as a "disgusting slob" who was "worthless and weak." Then he was blasted out the window of a second-story apartment. This theme of killing parents showed up regularly in the decade of the '80's. A group called Suicidal Tendencies released a recording in 1983 called "I Saw Your Mommy." Here is an excerpt of the gory lyrics:

**"I saw your mommy and your mommy's dead
I watched her as she bled
Chewed-off toes on her chopped-off feet
I took a picture because I thought it was neat
I saw your mommy and your mommy's dead
I saw her lying in a pool of red
I think it's the greatest thing I'll ever see___
Your dead mommy lying in front of me"**

For sheer banality, nothing yet produced can match "Momma's Gotta Die Tonight" by Body Count. The album sold 500,000 copies and featured its wretched lyrics on the CD jacket. Most of them are unfit to quote here, but they involved graphic descriptions of the rapper's mother being burned in her bed, then beaten to death with a baseball bat she had given him as a present, and finally the mutilation of the corpse into "little bitty pieces." What incredible violence! There was not a hint of guilt or remorse expressed by the rapper while telling us of this murder. In fact, he called his mother a "racist b---h," and laughed while chanting, "Burn, Momma, burn." My point is that the most popular music of our culture went from the inspiration of "Oh! My Papa" to the horrors of "Momma's Gotta Die Tonight" in scarcely more than a generation. And we have to wonder, where do we go from here?

As destructive and wicked as the youth culture is today, I must emphasize that these external influences will not explain all the rebellion that occurs in children (or in adults, for that matter). Why? Because we are free moral agents who are capable of independent choices and behavior. Psychologists have tried to convince us that human babies are born as "blank slates" on which the environment writes, and that we are nothing more than the sum total of our experiences. They have described us as unthinking responders who are "programmed" by what we see and hear. That is called "determinism," and it is wrong. I don't doubt that the world around us shapes and hones our personalities, but we arrive as infants with a temperament that is infinitely complex and unique from every other person on earth. We know from Scripture, and from more recent behavioral research, that there is something else------ operating from within ------ that interacts with environment to make us who we are. The human family inherits a sinful nature that is traced back to Adam's disobedience in the Garden of Eden.

43

Why is this understanding important to parents who are struggling with rebellious teenagers? Because it helps to explain why some kids with every advantage and opportunity do what is wrong, while others raised in terrible homes become pillars in the community. Children and young adults are capable of making choices that contradict everything they have been taught, and we as parents shouldn't be too quick to give ourselves the credit---------or the blame---------for everything they do......."

"Therefore, I hope you will resist the temptation to feel cheated or deprived because of the difficult temperament of your son or daughter. You are certainly not alone. In a survey of 3,000 parents, we found that 85 percent of families had at least one strong-willed child. So, you are not an exception or the butt of some cruel cosmic joke. This is parenthood. This is human nature. Most of us who have raised two or more kids have gone through some of the same stresses you are experiencing. We survived, and you will, too.

Think of it this way: You've been given a wonderful challenge as parents. You have the opportunity to guide these difficult kids through the mine fields of the '90's and bring them out on the other side of adolescence as responsible, loving adults. Anyone can raise the easy child. God has trusted you with a tougher assignment---and He will help you accomplish it.

Let me review the concepts we have considered and offer a few ideas that may be helpful:

1. You are not to blame for the temperament with which your child was born. He is simply a tough kid to handle, and your task is to rise to the challenge.

2. He is in greater danger because of his inclination to test the limits and scale the walls. Your utmost diligence and wisdom will be required to deal with him.

3. If you fail to understand his lust for power and independence, you can exhaust your resources and bog down in guilt. It will benefit no one.

4. If it is not already too late, by all means, take charge of your babies. Hold tightly to the reins of authority in the early days, and build an attitude of respect during your brief window of opportunity. You will need every ounce

of "awe" you can get during the years to come. Once you have established your right to lead begin to let go systematically, year by year.

5. Don't panic, even during the storms of adolescence. Better times are ahead. A radical turnaround usually occurs in the early 20s.

6. Stay on your child's team, even when it appears to be a losing team. You'll have the rest of your life to enjoy mutual fellowship if you don't overreact to frustration now.

7. Give him time to find himself, even if he appears not to be searching.

8. Most importantly, I urge you to hold your children before the Lord in fervent prayer throughout their years at home. I am convinced that there is no other source of confidence and wisdom in parenting. There is not enough knowledge in the book, mine or anyone else's, to counteract the evil that surrounds our kids today. Our teenagers are confronted by drugs, alcohol, sex, and foul language wherever they turn. And, of course, the peer pressure on them is enormous. We must bathe them in prayer every day of their lives. The God who made your children will hear your petitions. He has promised to do so. After all, He loves them more than you do."[1]

Pretty scary to read the lyrics on paper knowing they have only worsened since this letter was written! I was trying to relay to our son, that the lyrics do have an effect on our minds and that the enemy enters, through the things we listen to or watch. We need to guard our minds and fill them with only the things of the Lord.

The article made me feel better in some respects and worse in others because you see, our son continued to have problems that only intensified as the years went on, no matter what we did or said or how much help we tried to get.

We moved Rob from public school to private where the classrooms were smaller and where he could get some help with his learning disabilities. Things went pretty well for a period of time. The principal told us at the first sign of trouble; he would not be able to stay. It was very expensive for us to place him there and meant driving him across town twice a day, but we were willing to do anything we felt would help him.

He had not been there quite a year when he got into some trouble that got him expelled. We wanted so desperately to believe our son, and we sure didn't want him to have to leave the school, but we had no choice. Once again our hopes were dashed. We were at our wit's end. I have prayed for a very long time for someone to come along and be a spiritual mentor to him, someone he would listen to because he sure wasn't listening to us. Robbie had accepted Christ at age 9 and was baptized by my Dad at that time. Also at a revival he had gone down and rededicated himself and really seemed to be changing and expressed concern for some of his friends. We had some good times sharing spiritual things at that time, and I was so encouraged.

I had begun a prayer group for Mothers of prodigals, and our scripture at that first meeting was **Matthew 18:11-14 (NKJV),"The Son of Man has come to save that which was lost. What do you think? If a man has a hundred sheep, and one of them goes astray, does he not leave the ninety-nine and go to the mountains to seek the one that is straying? And if he should find it, assuredly, I say to you, he rejoices more over that sheep than over the ninety-nine that did not go astray. Even so it is not the will of your Father who is in heaven that on of these little ones should perish."**

We certainly had lost sheep, and we wanted to stand in the gap for them through prayer and to support each other through the pain and sorrow we felt. God was good to answer our prayers, and we saw some results from our time together. I was thumbing through the scripture and came to the passage in **Jeremiah 31:15-17 (NIV), "This is what the LORD said, A voice is heard in Ramah, mourning and great weeping, Rachel weeping for her children, and refusing to be comforted, because her children, are no more. This is what the LORD says: 'Restrain your voice from weeping and your eyes from tears; for your work shall be rewarded.' They shall return** from the land of the enemy. So there is hope for your future,' your children will return to their own land.'"

What an encouragement to me and a promise I believe God gave me for Robbie that He would bring him home from the enemy's territory. I just knew God was speaking to me through that scripture, and it has given me hope through these long years.

I am also reminded about the scripture which says in **Matthew 6:25 (NIV), "Therefore I tell you, do not worry about your life, what you will eat or what you will eat or drink, or about your body, what you will wear. Is not life more important than food, and the body more important than clothes? Look at the birds of the air; they do not sow or reap or store away in barns, and yet your heavenly Father feeds them. Are you not much more valuable than they? Who of you by worrying can add a single hour to his life?"**

And in **verse 33-34, "But seek first His kingdom and His righteousness, and all these things shall be added to you. Therefore do not worry about tomorrow, for tomorrow will worry about itself. Each day has enough trouble of its own."** I certainly felt at the time that I had sufficient troubles for the day!

It is so hard not to worry and just leave things in the Lord's hands. I so want to be in control and fix everything. God is teaching me every day that He is in control, and I am not.

I saw a picture one time of God on the throne and someone walking up the stairs to the throne and laying their burden down in His lap. Then they turned to walk back down the steps without a backward glance. I remember one lady, Lot's wife, who looked back and was turned into a pillar of salt. Ha, I am sure God has been tempted to do that to me many times.

I read **Ephesians 4:17-24 (NKJV)** to Robbie as a spiritual challenge. Paul wrote, **"This I say, therefore, and testify in the Lord, that you should no longer walk as the rest of the Gentiles walk, in the futility of their mind, having their understanding darkened, being alienated from the life of God, because of the ignorance that is in them, because of the blindness of their heart; who, being past feeling, have given themselves over to lewdness, to work all uncleanness with greediness. But you have not so learned Christ, if indeed you have heard Him and have been taught by Him, as the truth is in Jesus: that you put off, concerning your former conduct, the old man which grows corrupt according to the deceitful lusts, and be renewed in the spirit of your mind, and that you put on the new man which was created according to God, in true righteousness and holiness."**

I talked with him about what it meant to put off the old man and put on the new in Christ. It is a total transformation of what was in the old life and putting on the robe of Christ which symbolizes purity and holiness. We have to live our lives separated unto Him. We cannot serve two Masters, for we will either love the one or despise the other, but we cannot serve them at the same time. We need to strip off the old, filthy clothes of the world and replace them with the righteousness of Christ.

I also read him the passage in **Romans 7:21-24 (NIV)** which says, **"So I find this law at work: When I want to do good, evil is right there with me. For in my inner being I delight in God's law; but I see another law at work in the members of my body, waging war against the law of my mind and making me a prisoner of the law of sin at work within my members. What a wretched man I am!"** His comment was that that was the way he felt, wanting to do right but ultimately choosing to do wrong.

I was in the Christian bookstore one day and found a wonderful picture of the Shepherd reaching down over the edge of the cliff where the one lost sheep has fallen. He was reaching down to draw the sheep up into His arms. It was such a picture of God's love and concern over the lost sheep. He loved it so much that He left the other 99 to find the lost one. It gives me much hope for Robbie. I know God loves Robbie even more than I do, and I know He must grieve over him as I do. One day I pray I will see the Shepherd reach down that cliff and pull our lost sheep up, bandaging him up and bringing him home.

Here is a poem that Ruth Graham wrote in her book, <u>Prodigals and Those Who Love Them</u>:

For All Who Knew the Shelter of the Fold

"For all
who knew the shelter of The Fold,
its warmth and safety
and The Shepherd's care,
and bolted;
choosing instead to fare
out into the cold,
the night;
revolted
by guardianship,
by Light;
lured

by the unknown
eager to be out
and on their own;
freed
to water where they may,
feed
where they can,
live as they will:
till
they are cured,
let them be cold,
ill;
let them know terror;
feed
them with thistle,
weed,
and thorn;
who chose
the company of wolves,
let them taste
the company of wolves,
let them taste
the companionship wolves give
to helpless strays;
but, oh! Let them live---
wiser, though torn!
And wherever,
however, far away
they roam,
follow
and
watch
and
keep
Your stupid, wayward, stubborn
sheep
and someday
bring them Home!"[2]

I cried as I read this poem which I kept posted on my refrigerator for so many years. That was our prayer, not that he would just come back to his physical home, but home to the Father.

It is not easy to follow the advice in this passage not to lose heart, especially with so much going on with your child, when this affliction does not feel light, or when I am carrying a heavy load on my shoulders.

One night Robbie went to spend the night with a friend from school. I went in and checked things out and met the parents. We had entertained their son in our home several times. I felt comfortable letting him spend the night there. The next day I received a call from a fellow church member who had been at the YMCA and saw the sheriff arrest Robbie. It was his first experience with the law. We hired a lawyer and things came out okay, but we told him that it would be the first and last time we helped him with the law.

These days I try to stay in the Word just to keep myself from sinking. It gives me my very breath and ability to get through days of uncertainty.

I love the passage in **Psalm 69:1-3 (KJV), "Save me, O God! For the waters have come up to my neck. I sink in deep mire, where there is no standing; I have come into deep waters, where the floods overflow me. I am weary with my crying; my throat is dry; my eyes fail while I wait for my God."** That is often the way I feel, as if I am sinking under the floodwaters waiting on God to act on my behalf.

Job 2:2, 9-10 (NKJV) also speaks to me, **"And the Lord said to Satan, 'From where do you come?' So Satan answered the Lord and said,' from going to and fro on the earth, and from walking back and forth on it' Then his wife said to him, 'Do you still hold fast to your integrity? Curse God and die!' But he said to her, 'You speak as one of the foolish women speaks. Shall we indeed accept good from God, and shall we not accept adversity?'"**

I know Satan is certainly trying to devour our family. We will all face adversity. God uses it for His purposes and His glory. Can't you just see Satan walking to and fro before the throne of God asking permission to devour us? I am fighting with all the spiritual weapons I have in order to overcome Satan's plan with prayer and faith that the Father will rescue our son from the evil one.

Prayer: Lord, Help me not to lose heart. Remind me that these momentary afflictions are only for a little while compared to the weight of glory being produced in me for eternity. Thank you for your faithfulness in helping me to overcome the struggles of today. Help me to accept the hard things as well as the good, that come from Your hand. May I learn the lessons You intend for me to learn with each struggle in life, Amen.

CHAPTER FIVE

Lord, Forgive Me for My Judgmental Attitude

"DO NOT judge and criticize and condemn others, so that you may not be judged and criticized and condemned yourselves." Matthew 7:1, (AMP).

After just reading about the life of the Apostle Paul by Chuck Swindoll, I am almost embarrassed to say I have been through any trial compared to the beatings, persecutions, jail visits, ship wrecks, and finally the loss of his own life for the cause of Christ.

Also after having read Job many times I cannot say I have lost or suffered to the extent he did. I also just got through doing the study of John the Beloved by Beth Moore and was reminded of the sacrifice of the other disciples. I realize my difficulties seem trivial when they are compared to the glory of the cross.

My only hope is that sharing my struggles will minister to you and help you in some way or someone you love who has lost hope or feels all alone in their situation. Whatever heartache you are facing it is very real and personal to you. Don't ever say, "I shouldn't feel this way with my small problem compared to the one that seems so much bigger that someone else is struggling with, or worse yet let someone else tell you that. God knows what you can bear and He tests us in different ways and degrees.

Let's face it, none of us likes affliction. Paul didn't like the fact that he had infirmities and was anxious to get rid of them. He prayed three times for his thorn in the flesh to be removed but God chose not to answer his prayer the way he asked.

After facilitating the Bible Study, <u>Experiencing God</u>, which I referred to before, I found it was changing my spiritual life. I discovered that God is pursuing a love relationship with me and I had been so busy doing, and doing, for Him that I hadn't taken the time to really know Him.

I found out that that love relationship with Him is more important to Him and to me than anything else in the world. I was not having a consistent quiet time so I determined to begin that each morning. I would get up 15 minutes before I needed to get ready for work. Eventually that time grew and I was spending more time, more often searching the Word and seeking His direction for my life.

Things with Robbie, our son, continue to be a problem. I often became so weary, feeling I couldn't go on but God always encouraged me in His Word. I turned to **2 Corinthians 4:16-18 (NKJV), "Therefore we do not lose heart. Even though our outward man is perishing, yet the inward man is being renewed day by day. For our light affliction, which is but for a moment, is working for us a far more exceeding and eternal weight of glory, while we do not look at the things which are seen, but at the things which are not seen. For the things which are seen are temporary, but the things which are not seen are eternal."**

I must look beyond what my physical eyes are seeing to the spiritual, beyond the present to the future. I do believe God hears my prayer for Robbie and in His timing will bring him where he needs to be spiritually. I have to hold on to that hope or I will not make it.

It is hard to go into work each day with so much bearing down on me from home. I just don't know what to do but pray. I went to the prayer room at church after work one day and God took me to several scriptures. I am praying for endurance and for Robbie to be delivered from strongholds of drugs and alcohol. I want him to be free from all the devil is trying to tempt him with.

I was reading in **James 1:12-17 (NKJV), "Blessed is the man who endures temptation; for when he has been approved, he will receive the crown of life which the Lord has promised to those who love Him. Let no one say when he is tempted, "I was tempted by God", for God cannot be tempted by evil, nor does He Himself tempt anyone. But each one is tempted when he is drawn away by his own desires and enticed. Then, when desire has conceived, it gives birth to sin; and sin, when it is full-grown, brings forth death. Do not** be deceived, my beloved brethren. Every good gift and every perfect gift is from above, and comes down for the Father of lights, with whom there is no variation or shadow of turning."

The word temptation is better translated trial in this passage. In **verse 2-3** of the same chapter it says, **"My brethren, count it all joy when you fall into various trials, knowing that the testing of your faith produces patience."** Trials are those things that break the hope of joy, peace or tranquility in our lives. The reason for the test is to bring glory to God out of our struggles. God brings the trials into our lives sometimes to prove our faith.

It seems that we are being tested with all that is going on in Robbie's life. The question is, what will we learn through the testing? It is so hard to watch him going down the wrong path. He listens for a while and then is off doing his own thing the next thing we know.

I am very discouraged. What happened to all those promises you gave me Lord? When is it going to take place and when can I see Robbie serving you which is my heart's desire. Is all hope of deliverance gone?

Are the promises I felt I had from You just something I wanted to happen? Lord help me to see some glimpse of hope for the future. Am I worried about what others will say about my lack of control over my child or can I look at the full picture and Gods plan for Robbie's life? It all looks pretty grim. I feel like putting a paper bag over my head each time I go to church. I feel like everyone who knows anything about what we are dealing with are wondering why we can't get control.

How many times has God been disappointed in me? Yet He loves me unconditionally and promises to never leave me nor forsake me. Can I continue to love Robbie unconditionally? It hurts me so bad to see him making the wrong choices. I felt like telling him if he wants to continue to drink and do drugs he will have to find somewhere else to live because I cannot watch him destroy himself. If that is what he wants to do--he is free to go, but it would break my heart to see him make that choice, so right now I cannot say that to him.

In my quiet time the next morning I read an article in the In Touch Magazine by Charles Stanley which helped me:

> "God has a unique plan for your life, one that does not change according to circumstance, environment, public opinion, or secret fears. When you confront a situation that does not line up with your understanding of how God wants your life to proceed, you are forced to stop and look at Him for direction. Sometimes God allows you to

be disappointed in personal expectations so that you will learn to rely on Him more fully, to walk by faith and not by human sight."[1]

I read Hebrews 11 about the people of faith and what faith is: It is the substance of things hoped for, the evidence of things not seen. By faith Abraham obeyed, by faith Abraham, when he was tested, offered up Isaac, by faith they passed through the Red Sea, by faith the walls of Jericho fell down, and by faith the harlot Rahab did not perish. Where is my faith now? Do I have faith to believe God for His promises?

I love the passage in **Romans 4:3 (NKJV)** which says, **"For what does the scripture say? Abraham believed God, and it was accounted to him for righteousness."** I believe Lord that you will work that miracle I am praying for in Your own time and in Your own way. You want to accomplish the things you have planned both in Robbie and us as his family for Your honor and for Your glory and I choose to trust you for it.

I wrote in my journal today that I was feeling really down. I can't shake the feeling of oppression. I feel like running away. What is the passage in **Psalm 55:6 (NKJV), "Oh, that I had wings like a dove! For then I would fly away and be at rest."** That is what I would like to do!

Jimmy and I had a disagreement over an issue regarding Robbie. I get so tired of being in the middle sometimes. Lord, I'm ready for a closing to this chapter in our lives. I need to see something miraculous happen. Or, I need you to give me a word of promise from your word to see me through. It gets hard to keep going on sometimes.

In my reading today I came across the passage in **Matthew 19:26 (NKJV), But Jesus looked at them and said to them, "With men this is impossible, but with God all things are possible."** Praise Him for reminding me all things are possible with Him.

Robbie is not abiding by the house rules, staying out late at night, etc. Jimmy says he is going to tell him tonight that he can't live here any longer. It was a real bad scene. As I shared before, even though I know it has to be done in my head, my heart is breaking and I don't know where he will go. Robbie went down and packed his clothes and had a friend pick him up. I went out to the car with him and cried till I felt like my heart would literally break. It felt as if my heart was being squeezed in a vise. I was so distraught and angry with Jimmy and the circumstances so I went on to bed and tried to escape the world with sleep.

I have not placed my finger on what drew Robbie into the drug scene but some of the issues mentioned in an article I once read, have certainly been problems with him. Due to the LD and ADHD he had suffered from low self-esteem and insecurities. No matter how many times we told him that some folks just had to learn in a different manner and needed extra help, he found it hard to accept. He felt poorly about himself and his abilities.

I believe Robbie's feeling of not fitting in turned to anger, hurt, and loneliness. He has a void that can only be filled with the love and compassion of the Heavenly Father. We have tried to show love to him in every way we could but it never seemed to be enough. He always needed more reassurance for some reason.

Robbie is like the prodigal son in the Bible. The word prodigal means "extravagant, someone who is lavish with his or her resources, recklessly wasteful, someone who is a spendthrift". I can feel the pain and agony the Father experienced when the prodigal left home. I use to pray to the Lord to take Robbie on home with Him if his life would be in continuous rebellion, because I felt he was God's child.

Instead, God has protected him many times. He was in an accident one time when he was drinking and had a buddy in the car with him. He was running away from the police because he knew he would get charged if caught. He was going so fast that he lost control in the curve and flipped head over heels and landed upside down. The police told us at the hospital that they had thought that they would need a coroner, not an ambulance.

Another time he was in a wreck and ran off down in a field and had slight injuries. I am sure there were many times we don't even know about where God's protection was on him. I sometimes wondered if my prayers got above my head but I know God heard the cries of a desperate Mother for protection for her son. I just praise the Lord that in those accidents no one was severely hurt or injured. Neither time was another car involved when these accidents occurred.

In the book, <u>Surviving the Prodigals in your life</u>, written by Woodrow Kroll, I came to something I found very interesting and want to share with you parents who might be dealing with a prodigal.

> "When a teen decides he or she doesn't want to live at home anymore and leaves the parents without a trace, that teen is responsible for his or her own actions. When

a man leaves his wife and kids to take up with some gal at the office, that husband is responsible for his own actions. We have to begin acting like adults; we have to begin to take responsibility for our actions.

Regardless of how you as a parent or spouse may have contributed to the troubles of your prodigal, there is an underlying truth that surfaces in the parable of the prodigal son. The lad was responsible for what happened to him after he left home. He was on his own and he was responsible.

But there is another equally important truth wedded to the first in this story—a truth for all those waiting the return of prodigals. Here it is: You are not the object of your spouse's prodigalism. You are not the object of your son or daughter's anger. You may feel it keenly, but if you're to survive the prodigals in your life, you must recognize that their prodigalism is directed toward someone else, not primarily toward you. Prodigalism, like all other sin, is ultimately always directed against God.

In the prodigals confession he said, "Father, I have sinned against heaven and against you." Heaven first, father second.

If you're battling feelings of guilt because you have a prodigal in your family, remember this: Sin is, ultimately, always directed against God. When your prodigal sins against you, it's not really you they are directing their vengeance toward, they are sinning against God. That's what makes it sin---it's ultimately always directed against God. When we sin, do we involve other people? Frequently we do, but we always involve God. When we sin, do we hurt other people? Yes we do, but we ultimately hurt our Heavenly Father. In the final analysis, sin is always directed against God."[2]

The elder brother could not believe that his father was welcoming the prodigal son home with a party. He approached his father with anger and bitterness.

That is one of the many things I can say about our daughter, Melissa. She was always been very concerned about her brother and was always ready to welcome him home. It made her angry that he was doing what he was to himself and to us and she told him so many times, but she has always been forgiving and loving. We thank the Father for her compassion, love and forgiving spirit. She is truly a jewel. Forgive us Melissa because I know there were times we failed you in our efforts to help your brother.

Melissa and I have talked about how much Robbie has taught us on this family journey. One of those lessons is conviction of our judgmental attitudes in regards to the way people dress, or if they didn't act the way we felt they should. God often shows folks to us so we can intercede on their behalf, not judge them.

In **1 Samuel 16:7 (AMP)** it says, **"But the Lord said to Samuel, 'Look not on his appearance, or at the height of his stature, for I have not rejected him; for the Lord sees not as man sees; for man looks on the outward appearance, but the Lord looks on the heart."**

I don't know what kind of background you come from, whether rich or poor, from a Christian home or having never attended church, functional, dysfunctional, or whatever. But I do know whatever background you emerged from you have come away with some sort of judgmental attitude.

I found myself judging folks for what they wore and what they did according to my set of standards. I would even look down on them and really regarded them as lost and going to hell in some instances.

Oh, if we would ever learn that God looks on the heart, not the outward appearance. I have met many that at first glance appeared to be very beautiful outwardly but once you really got to know them your perspective changed dramatically because what is in the heart eventually finds its way out.

Then again, someone who may not look as pleasant outwardly you learn has a heart of gold. I was guilty of snide comments when someone went by dressed different from myself, wearing tattoos, men with long hair or ear rings, dirty and unkempt, different color hair like blue, green, etc.

Now I ask the Father to let me see them through His eyes. Just because someone doesn't dress or respond to life in the way I would does not mean they are lost. We have an ex-biker in our church that is working with the prison ministry and wears jeans and a leather vest most of the time. He has long hair and many tattoos. He is able to minister to those bikers and prisoners in a way that someone wearing a suit and tie may not. Just seeing him dressed in that manner gives some that common ground but they can also see Jesus flowing from his inner man and know he is different because of Who lives within him.

Have you ever been quick to judge someone because of the choices they made or decisions they made that are different from what you would have done? Or have you ever said things or thought things like, "I would never do that or my children would never act like that or make any wrong choices in life?

I have, and I had to eat those words and they tasted real bad coming up and I found it hard to swallow them back down. We as "Christians" can be the cruelest to our fellow brothers and sisters in Christ. Let someone fall and instead of restoring them in love as the Word instructs us, we condemn them, gossip about them (maybe even requesting prayer for them in order to let others know the situation), or worse ignore them. We are sometimes so filled with pride that we honestly don't think we could fall into those same temptations. Sometimes along the way we may fall prey to the same sin or worse. The word says, Be careful lest you fall into the same temptation. We are all capable of doing some pretty bad things if push comes to shove. We think we could never kill anyone but we do it daily with our words.

I have often wondered what we would do if a prostitute, transvestite, homeless person, drunkard, or someone who maybe had not had a bath recently sat down beside us in our modern day churches, how would we respond? Would we show them love and graciousness as Christ would do and have us to do, or would we look down our self righteous noses at them. We forget we are sinners ourselves, saved by grace. But by the grace of God there go I.

When in Africa I had a true test of this. Several of us piled into a van to go back to our hotel with the nationals and it was hot and sticky and we were tired. As I sat there I breathed a word of prayer for the Father to make the air smell of His fragrance in our nostrils and you know He did! I pray now everyday that I will be a pleasant fragrance in His nostrils as I go about my daily walk. He shows me daily how far I have to go but praise Him He is showing me my evil wicked heart. As hard as it is to see my heart, I am grateful He loves me enough to change it.

Prayer: Lord, help me to endure this time in my life. I pray you will deliver Robbie from the stronghold of drugs and alcohol. Do whatever it takes to bring him back into the fold. Protect his life Lord and put Your hedge of protection around him but teach him Lord, Amen

CHAPTER SIX

Our Son's First Arrest

"Wine is a mocker. Strong drink is a brawler; whoever is led astray by them is not wise." Proverbs 20:1, (NIV).

Although God provides courage and strength for our journey, our lives continue to be torn apart with worry, and yes sometimes hopelessness, over the sinful choices in our son's life. He continues to party and drink. Our parental instruction and warnings of destruction for the party life apparently make no difference to Robbie.

One morning God led me to **Proverbs 19:18-19 (NKJV), "Chasten your son while there is hope, and do not set your heart on his destruction. A man of great wrath will suffer punishment; for if you rescue him, you will have to do it again." Proverbs 3:11 (NKJV),"My son, do not despise the chastening of the LORD, nor detest His correction; for whom the LORD loves He corrects, Just as a father the son in whom he delights."** It is interesting that I would come to these passages after our discussion with Robbie about the dangers of alcohol.

God sent me a word through a friend from **Jeremiah 1:19 (NKJV)," 'They will fight against you, but they shall not prevail against you. For I am with you,' says the Lord, 'to deliver you'."**

I am reminded that "we wrestle not with flesh and blood, but ... against spiritual wickedness" which is my paraphrase from Ephesians 6:12. It is not the person we are wrestling against; it is the enemy using that person for his purposes. I must remind myself of this fact often. Man is not my enemy; the devil is. I know Robbie has given Satan a foothold in his life through alcohol and other drugs and by what he watches and listens to. If I can see beyond the actions of the person I am dealing with to who is behind his actions, I can handle situations much better. Then I can stand firm on the promises of God and stand in the gap prayerfully for Robbie to be delivered from the strongholds of the devil.

We got a call from Robbie telling us he was in jail. He had been arrested for drinking under age at a party he attended and causing a disturbance. I went to the jail to see him after work that next day. I could not believe that I was going to visit my son in jail. Never in my wildest dreams did I imagine jail would be a possibility. My prayers had been that God would stop him before it came to this, but I remembered my prayer, whatever it took.

I had to stand outside a door which had a small glass window and a speaker box to talk to him. On that first visit neither he nor I could talk for the tears streaming down our faces. He was dressed in an orange jumpsuit and looked so helpless and afraid. Lord, this is just so hard.

So many look at the actions of the accused and proclaim they deserve it, but at the same time, the family of the offender also suffers from the consequences, and for the first time I see how true that is. We tend not to consider the heartache of the family involved, and many times we proclaim it must be because of the way he was raised. So many like myself ask, "How could this happen? I've tried to teach and demonstrate the love of the Lord to my children, and yet he or she chose to go astray."

Not everyone has the opportunity to be raised in a home which teaches the things of the Lord. Many don't even know who their fathers are. Some have been abandoned by their own mothers. Some were raised in homes where drugs and alcohol were readily available, and so the curse is passed to the sons and daughters. So why have some chosen to run away from the things they were taught? They were in actuality running from God as Woodrow Kroll stated in his book. Yet some came out of the worst of homes and lived their lives to honor the Father. They chose the better road for their lives. Who can figure it out?

We can't do what is right in our own strength; we need the strength of the Lord. **"I can do all things through Christ who strengthens me."**

Philippians 4:13 (NKJV) says. This is where Satan attacks us. We forget where our strength comes from and begin thinking we can do it on our own.

At this point Robbie had 30 days to serve, so I prayed this would get his attention and that he would walk the right path when he got out. There are lots of folks praying for him. We prayed against the wrong influences and friends in his life. We also prayed God's mercy on his life.

One morning I came to the passage in **II Chronicles 16: 9 (NKJV), "For the eyes of the Lord run to and fro throughout the whole earth, to show Himself strong on behalf of those whose heart is loyal to Him."** Oh Lord, I want to be found loyal to You. Teach me your ways. I desire my children remain loyal in all their ways and affections to You, Lord, so You will bless them and their lives will glorify You.

Isaiah 57:17-18 (NKJV) promises, **"For the iniquity of his covetousness I was angry and struck him; I hid and was angry, and he went on backsliding in the way of his heart. I have seen his ways, and will heal him; I will also lead him, and restore comforts to him and to his mourners."** That gave me encouragement that God is promising healing to the ones who willfully go their own way. Lord, I pray that You will bring revival to Robbie's soul and that it will be soon.

At this same time my husband, Jimmy, also began struggling with what to do about his job situation. He was passed over for a job promotion, and the new boss started making things difficult. The boss wanted Jimmy out of the office, so he sent Jimmy on the road traveling. We began to see the writing on the wall.

My Dad shared with us that Jimmy is now in the lions' den, but he has God's protection while in there. He also reminded us that the ones who threw Daniel in were thrown in afterwards, and the lions devoured them before their feet hit the bottom. The Lord was on our side as we sought His direction.

While away at the beach, Jimmy and I prayed about the job situation, and Jimmy confessed that his motives toward his boss were not pure. I also found myself in the boss's office one day upon our return apologizing for my wrong attitude and actions towards him. It was hard to do but I knew God had convicted me because I was His representative and had acted wrongly. I needed to make things right.

Sometimes God has us do some tough things, but if we are obedient, He brings us peace. Shortly thereafter, Jimmy was removed from the lions' den and given a promotion to a different job. This, too, kept us in the crucible. The battles we faced were the Lord's and we were to take our battle position and see Him work.

Prayer: Lord, some days I am so weary from waiting for your promises to manifest themselves in my life, but I continue to trust You. I don't even have the words I need today, Amen.

CHAPTER SEVEN

Our First Visit to Prison

James 5:19-20, (TLB) issues this challenge to us, **"Dear brothers, if anyone has slipped away from God and no longer trusts the Lord, and someone helps him understand the Truth again, that person who brings him back to God will have saved a wandering soul from death, bringing about the forgiveness of his many sins."**

We sometimes do write those off who have sinned by feeling prideful that we have not fallen into that particular sin. Lord, forgive me when I fail in this matter.

Allow me to give you a word of encouragement once again if you have greatly failed in an important area of your life. I think of David and how he succumbed to the temptation of Bathsheba as she bathed across the way. (What in the world was she doing bathing out on that balcony anyway?) Oh well, we know the story, he did not resist but lay with her, and she became pregnant. David admitted to Nathan that he had sinned and confessed his sin before the Father.

In Psalm 51 it gives a detailed account of his sorrow for his sin. He confessed and turned from his sin and prayed for the Lord to restore the joy of his salvation. Not his salvation but the *joy* of his salvation. God did restore him, but there were consequences for the sin. He lost his newborn son among many others, but God used him in a mighty way as king in the land.

I think of Peter who, given the test of acknowledging His connection with the Lord, denied he even knew Him. God had already told him he would deny Him, but Peter did not believe it until the cock crowed. Peter went away ashamed, but God restored him and called him the rock on which he built His church.

My point is that God does give second chances. He does not cut someone off from service and usefulness if they will confess their sins. In fact, God promises that **"If we confess our sins, he is faithful and just and will forgive us our sins and purify us from all unrighteousness," I John 1:9 (NIV).**

Some of course, are not repentant and continue on in their rebellion against God. Homes are destroyed, and lives are eternally changed.

In our prayer time under the pulpit on Sunday we talked about and prayed about laying our Isaacs on the altar. Is God calling me to lay my Isaac down? Of course, I am referring to the account in Hebrews 11 which states, **"By faith Abraham, when he was tested, offered up Isaac, and he who had received the promises offered up his only begotten son, of whom it was said, 'In Isaac your seed shall be called,' accounting that God was able to raise him up, even from the dead, from which he also received him in a figurative sense" (NKJV).**

Genesis 22:1 says, "After these things.... God tested Abraham." The faith of Abraham has always amazed me as he ventured out toward the mountain to be obedient to the command of God. I can just imagine the thoughts going through his head and the thoughts of Isaac as he asked his father where the sacrificial lamb was. Isaac walked on with his father in complete trust.

Can you imagine the pain Abraham experienced as he took that knife in his hand to bring down on his only begotten son? The son through whom was promised a whole nation? What faith it took, and **"it was accounted to him as righteousness because he believed God,"** as stated in **Romans 4:3.**

Abraham proved his love for his heavenly Father over the love he had for his son. Is there someone in your life who seems to be more important to you than your heavenly Father? God may just test you to see. He is a jealous God and does not want us to have anyone or anything before Him. Anything or anyone we place before Him is considered an idol and will have to be torn down.

In **Deuteronomy 4:24 (NKJV)** it says, **"For the LORD your God is a consuming fire, a jealous God."** He will not allow another to have the glory due His name. In **Isaiah 42:8 (NKJV)** it says, **"I am the LORD, that is My name; and My glory I will not give to another, nor My praise to carved images."** Exodus 34:14 (NKJV) proclaims, **"For you shall worship no other god, for the LORD, whose name is Jealous, is a jealous God."**

In my time alone with the Lord this morning I was reading in **Luke 14:26 (NKJV)** which says, **"If anyone comes to Me and does not hate his father and mother, wife and children, brothers and sisters, yes, and his own life also, he cannot be My disciple."** Oh I want to be obedient to His call even when it takes me away from my family for a time. I remember reading from Henry Blackaby's writings not to refuse to obey what you know God has called you to do because you fear the cost too great to your family.

Robbie was once again on probation. He had broken his probation requirements, and he called to say that he will turn himself in tomorrow. He wants us to come get him at his friend's house and let him stay the night, so we did and spent the night sharing our hearts. The next day I took him to the sheriff's office. As we sat in the lobby waiting on the sheriff, there were three boys who were also waiting and asked us why we were there. Robbie told them, "to turn himself in". One of them encouraged him to run before they got there to take him in. I knew it was the voice of the enemy. Robbie literally put his hands over his ears and refused to listen. I was so proud of him for that. He said he was doing the right thing.

As the sheriff arrived to take Robbie down to the magistrate's office, he instructed me to follow them. I told him I was not going to post bond. He seemed very surprised. He placed the handcuffs on Robbie and placed him in the car to take him to the jail. It is so painful to watch him going off, but I know it must be done. I feel I have placed my Isaac on the altar. He is not innocent as Isaac was so God will have to discipline him for his actions. **Psalm 119:71 (AMP), "It is good for me that I have been afflicted, that I might learn Your statutes."** Robbie needs to learn God's statutes. There is no sacrificial lamb to take his place, although we know as believers that our Lamb sacrificed His own life for our sakes, and His blood covers our sins.

I went home and tried to stay busy and do chores to keep my mind off the events of the day, but Robbie was in my every thought and prayer. I prayed for his protection and for God's mercy. I know to stay in the Word which told me in **Ephesians 5:20 (KJV), "Giving thanks always for all things unto God and the Father in the name of our Lord Jesus Christ."**

It is oftentimes hard to give thanks for the things that bring us such pain and heartache.

The next day put a new slant on things. Robbie called begging me to come and get him out. He said the inmates were threatening him. I talked to the supervisor at the jail, and he assured me that he would check out the unit he was in to see what was going on. I hope I can trust him to do what he promised. I felt this was another test.

God reminded me of **II Chronicles 20:12, 15b, 17, 18b (NKJV)** once again, **"O our God, will You not judge them? For we have no power against this great multitude that is coming against us; nor do we know what to do, but our eyes are upon You. Do not be afraid nor dismayed because of this great multitude, for the battle is not yours, but God's. You will not need to fight in this battle. Position yourselves, stand still and see the salvation of the LORD, who is with you, O Judah and Jerusalem! Do not fear or be dismayed; tomorrow go out against them, for the LORD is with you. And the inhabitants of Jerusalem bowed before the LORD, worshipping the LORD."**

We must worship and praise the Lord even in our trying circumstances, taking our battle position in worship and praise to the Father as He fights our battles. The people were so sure of God's promise of victory that they started praising and singing even before the battle began. This was God's instruction to me.

I went to visit Robbie. As I walked the long hallway, I became sick to my stomach, not believing that I was coming to this place to see my son once again. We had to see each other through another glass enclosure with a phone on the wall to talk through. He and I both cried once again through our visit. He did not want me to leave. He reminded me of the little boy he once was as he came to me with his hurts and wanted me to hold him.

In **1 Kings 8:56b (AMP)** it says, **"Not one word has failed of all His good promise which He promised."** Thank You for this reminder Lord because some days it looks like Your promises are failing because I am not seeing what I want to see in Robbie. I know You do not lie.

It is hard to say, but in some ways we feel more peace when Robbie is behind bars and not able to run around doing things we worry about. I stay upset when he is out thinking we might get a call saying he has been in some accident or has overdosed or that the sheriff will once again show up at our door telling us something horrible. At least we know where he is right now, no matter how painful it is.

Robbie asked another inmate to call us saying he was in the pit or hole as they call it. It is solitary confinement. They are placed in a cell by themselves for 23 hours with only one hour to come out and bathe and stretch. He is begging us to get him out again. It puts me in such agony. I know we are doing the right thing, so I go to the Word for comfort and solace. I will have to stop answering the phone as hard as that is for now.

The Lord comforted me with **Psalm 130:1-5 (NKJV), "Out of the depths I have cried to You, O LORD; Lord, hear my voice! Let Your ears be attentive to the voice of my supplications. If You, LORD, should mark iniquities, O Lord, who could stand? But there is forgiveness with You, that You may be feared. I wait for the LORD, my soul waits, and in His word I do hope."**

Psalm 107: 10-20 (NKJV) says, " **Those who sat in darkness and in the shadow of death, bound in affliction and irons-because they rebelled against the words of God, and despised the counsel of the Most High, therefore He brought down their heart with labor; they fell down, and there was none to help. Then they cried out to the LORD in their trouble, and He saved them out of their distresses. He brought them out of darkness and the shadow of death, and broke their chains in pieces. Oh, that men would give thanks to the LORD for his goodness, and for His wonderful works to the children of men! For He has broken the gates of bronze, and cut the bars of iron in two. Fools, because of their transgression, and because of their iniquities, were afflicted. Their soul abhorred all manner of food, and they drew near to the gates of death. Then they cried out to the LORD in their trouble, and He saved them out of their distresses. He sent His word and healed them, and delivered them from their destructions."**

It is my prayer that Robbie will cry out in his distress and that God will bring him out of the darkness into the light. The Lord wants Robbie to cry out for Him and receive what He has for him to do. We can't serve two masters as he has been trying to do.

Once again I feel as if my heart is in a vise and someone is tightening it little by little. It is so hard to wait on the Lord. I feel Robbie is thinking we have deserted him, and I know he does not like us right now. Oh God, help him to understand that we love him and are trying to work all things for his good through obedience to You in this matter.

Praise You, Lord, that when we cry out you will not totally consume us or forsake us. I know You are in that jail cell with Robbie. You see his heart and understand him so much better than we do. You know his every need.

My spiritual mentor gave me **Nahum 1:3a (NKJV), "The Lord is slow to anger and great in power."** God's love is very deep, and Rob's misery is God's mercy.

Rob called again. He said he is still in the pit or hole and that his hair is falling out, he feels he is going crazy, he is not eating and is blue from the air conditioning. He says they take his mattress and blanket at 8:00 a. m. and don't give it back until 11 p.m. He continues to ask me to come get him. The whole thing upsets me so much, but I have my instructions from the Lord not to rescue him, and I won't. I have intervened far too many times already. He is the Lord's and as hard as the prayer is to pray, we pray, "Whatever it takes, You do it, Lord. Your hand is much kinder and more merciful than anyone else."

Robbie is finally out of the pit and in a cell alone at this point, which he likes. He sounds so much stronger and better than before. Thank you for that gift, Lord. He is scheduled to go before the judge and we are praying God's will in the situation. We have a business trip to Pinehurst, and Jimmy will be receiving an award, so we will depend on Robbie to call my parents with the results. I have this feeling in my spirit that he will do some time in prison this time.

When I called and talked to my Mother, I can sense it is not good news. He received ten months. My Mother is quite upset as we talked, but I believed God meant it for Robbie's good. He has a purpose in it, and we must trust Him.

As we celebrated the birthday of our son-in-law, Bryan, Melissa suggested that we save a napkin and plate from each gathering and share them with Robbie in a great big party when he comes home. Once again she demonstrated her loving and compassionate spirit. We praise God for her beautiful heart. Once again, she bears no resemblance to the older brother in the prodigal son story.

We visited Robbie for the first time in a prison setting. The place is surrounded by two rows of barbed wire. I can't believe our son is in surroundings such as these. Never in a million years did I believe I would have to see him this way, jail was bad enough! Sometimes it is good when we don't know what is ahead because we might not be able to make it.

We sat in the large waiting area to see him and when he came in he just fell into my arms, and we cried a while. He appeared to be broken. He did the same with his Dad and it was hard for him to get out the words, "Happy Fathers Day," but he managed. He was very emotional as we visited and especially as we prepared to leave. It was the most helpless feeling when we heard those prison doors close knowing we were leaving our son behind.

I had **Lamentations 3: 19-36 (NKJV)** for Rob. "**Remember my affliction and roaming, the wormwood and the gall. My soul still remembers and sinks within me. This I recall to my mind, therefore I have hope. Through the LORD's mercies we are not consumed, because His compassions fail not. They are new every morning; great is Your faithfulness. 'The LORD is my portion,' says my soul, 'therefore I hope in Him!' The LORD is good to those who wait for Him, to the soul who seeks Him. It is good that one should hope and wait quietly for the salvation of the LORD. It is good for a man to bear the yoke in his youth. Let him sit alone and keep silent, because God has laid it on him; let him put his mouth in the dust-there may yet be hope. Let him give his cheek to the one who strikes him, and be full of reproach. For the Lord will not cast off forever. Though He causes grief, yet He will show compassion according to the multitude of His mercies. For He does not afflict willingly, nor grieve the children of men. To crush under one's feet all the prisoners of the earth, to turn aside the justice due a man before the face of the Most High, or subvert a man in his cause---The Lord does not approve.**" These were my words of hope and comfort as I prayed for my troubled son.

Prayer: I thank you Lord for your discipline which shows Your deep love for Your wayward children. We know that it is not Your desire to afflict, but I believe You have answered my prayer as I cried out for You to do whatever it took to bring Robbie to his senses. I pray this time away to think will cause our son to begin his journey back to You, Amen.

CHAPTER EIGHT

Family Tragedy

"Weeping may endure for the night, but joy comes in the morning." Psalm 30:5b, (AMP).

One evening as we sat watching TV, we received a call from Jimmy's mother saying that his uncle, "Chief", had been found dead, and apparently murdered. His friend who had missed seeing him noticed for two or three days that his papers were in the driveway. The authorities were called in and found him in his bedroom which had been burned pretty badly. We were all in shock.

We went down to help to make some funeral arrangements for him as he had no other family but us. His wife had passed away years before with cancer, and he had moved to help take care of his mother until her death.

We all met at the funeral home, and the arrangements were made according to what the family felt he would have wanted. We went to get a bite of supper as we left the funeral home. After eating, my father-in-law got up and quickly sat back down stating he didn't feel well.

He slumped over, and I pulled him to the floor to begin CPR. I remember crying out to the Lord to spare his life. Jimmy's mother had already left that area of the restaurant because she was so upset. She didn't need any more bad news at this point. As the rescue squad arrived, I began to see the life come back into his body. They took him to the hospital and determined he had congestive heart failure. He would remain in the hospital for a day or two but wanted to go to the funeral service.

I wrote the following entry into my journal: "This journal is full of pain and sorrow, and I am not sure a lot of restoring has begun, but I know God has sustained us through each and every step and that He will do so to the end. He has truly given me peace that surpasses all understanding even through the hardest times."

Chief was buried, but the memories of his life will go on forever due to his generous contributions to many lives. He is at peace and at home with his Heavenly Father, in a greater place than we are on this earth.

I am reminded again of the passage in **Psalm 30:5b (AMP), "Weeping may endure for a night, but joy comes in the morning."** Any man can sing in the light moments when all is well, but only if you have seen God work in those trying times can you truly know the joy of the Lord and be able to sing His praises even in the dark hours of your life. This chapter of our lives is no different.

I need a word from the Lord each day because I've learned that I don't know what each day might hold. I might need to share that word with someone else to bring encouragement and hope in the midst of their pain during my day or I might need it myself. That is why I get up so early to have that time with my Father in preparation for my day.

As a nurse I work in an area preparing folks for surgery. Sometimes that surgery is going to determine whether the person has cancer or some other dreaded diagnosis. The patient and their families are very anxious at this time and may come across as angry or rude. I have to be well-grounded in the Word so I won't react to them in that same manner. I want to be a nurse getting all the facts straight but also attending to the needs of the patients and families, whether they are physical, emotional, or spiritual needs. I have to be ready to share the hope that is within me.

It is so amazing how God brings particular folks to me who are dealing with or have recently dealt with some of the same issues I have. This brings instant camaraderie. I can't spend a great deal of time conversing, but God protects my time with the individual person as He sees fit. I look on my position not only as a job but as an assignment from God to share with those He brings my way. In light of that, He gives me many divine appointments. I praise Him for each one and pray I will respond in a manner with which He will be pleased. Sometimes His assignments are tough and I struggle with those tasks, but if I want to be in good fellowship with Him I must obey His call.

One day while attempting to discern His direction, He spoke to my spirit through a devotional and asked if I was more afraid of what man thought or what He thought! That spurred me on to follow through with His assignment. It is not always popular with man, but always wise to follow His leading.

> *Prayer: Thank you for walking with us again in the face of trial and loss. I love You Lord. Thank You for holding my right hand. Thank You for divine appointments and continue to teach me to follow Your direction as You bring those divine appointments my way, Amen.*

CHAPTER NINE

Struggles Through Guillian-Barre Syndrome

"Go imprison yourself in your house, and I will paralyze you so you can't leave." Ezekiel 3:24b-25, (TLB).

One bright beautiful day my husband, Jimmy, and I were walking in the neighborhood. We were discussing the trials we had endured in our life together. We recalled how faithful God had been to see us through each one. But to be honest, we were beginning to feel like maybe Job's last name was Kearns! Not that we had experienced all Job had, but we had been through a lot. I made the statement that at least we had our health. As Jimmy likes to tell it, I continued to have mine, he did not.

Four or five days later on a Monday night, Jimmy was washing his truck. He came upstairs telling me he felt like he could not even grip the sponge he was using to wash the truck. He had played five hours of tennis the weekend before, so we just surmised his hand and arm were tired and really didn't think any more about it.

The next day Jimmy and I went to work, but I decided to call him later in the day to see how he was feeling. He said that his whole arm felt weaker. I insisted he leave work and go to see our family physician. I called and made him an appointment for that same afternoon. At the examination the doctor confirmed that he had just probably overdone himself over the weekend and gave him some anti-inflammatory drugs and sent him home.

We went to a tennis tournament being played in town that evening, and Jimmy felt like he was okay. I decided to drive home, to give him some rest. As we arrived home Jimmy reached down to get something that had dropped onto the floor board, and while leaning on his hand for support, it gave way. He ended up face down in the floor because he had lost his strength.

The next morning in my quiet time God took me to **Ezekiel 3:24b-25 (TLB)**. I was reading the Living Bible version which read, **"Go imprison yourself in your house, and I will paralyze you so you can't leave."** I knew in my spirit that God was telling me that Jimmy was going to be paralyzed! I had learned to hear the Shepherd's voice by this time, so I knew He was preparing me. I remember slamming my Bible shut and crying out, "Oh Lord, no."

I did not tell Jimmy at the time what I had read. As he arose to prepare for work, I went to the kitchen to make coffee and took it to him. He said, "I need you to help me dry off because I don't seem to have the strength to do it myself." That really concerned me. I knew something was dreadfully wrong. Jimmy was determined he was going to work, so I helped him dress. He got in the car and drove to the end of the driveway and could hardly change the gears in the car, and as he later told me, he could not get the seatbelt fastened.

Finally, as I watched him from the front porch, he shook his head, put the car in drive, and drove back toward the house. He got out of the car saying, "I can't drive." At this point I couldn't help but reflect on the passage I had read earlier. I went inside and called our doctor at home and told him that something was definitely wrong. He instructed me to have Jimmy up at his office as soon as possible.

After a brief examination he told us he would like for us to go and see a neurologist. We went to see Dr. Jackson, and he did an examination and asked lots of questions. The doctor told us he thought we might be dealing with Guillain-Barre' Syndrome. Then he sent us directly to the hospital to be admitted for more tests. We were sitting in chairs, giving our information to the clerk, and as she finished, Jimmy started to stand but could hardly muster up the strength to walk. The personnel decided to take him upstairs in a wheelchair. I stayed and got Jimmy settled in and then went home to pack some clothes and personal items for him to have for his stay in the hospital.

The next morning he called and told me that he got up to go to the bathroom in the middle of the night and fell to the floor. The nursing personnel had to pick him up and carry him back to bed. He was now at the point that he could hardly move his hands and arms. He was not progressing in the typical way Guillain-Barre Syndrome usually exhibited itself, so they were testing for all kinds of things, like Lou Gehrig's, muscular dystrophy, or myasthenia's gravis.

On Thursday he was officially diagnosed with Guillain-Barre Syndrome after much testing and deliberations. The doctors suggested he receive seven plasma phoresis treatments which are like a cleansing of the blood. The plan was to give him one a day. It doesn't cure the disease but stops it from progressing.

The syndrome is a rare illness that affects the peripheral nerves of the body. It can cause weakness and paralysis, as well as abnormal sensations. The syndrome occurs sporadically, that is, it cannot be predicted, and can occur at any age and to both sexes.

It can vary greatly in severity from the mildest case, which may not even be brought to the doctors' attention, to a devastating illness with almost complete paralysis that brings a patient close to death. Because it is so rare, most of the public has never heard of the illness. Yet, for those affected, the illness can be severely disabling.

The cause of Guillain-Barre Syndrome is not known. A variety of events seem to trigger the illness. Many cases occur a few days to a few weeks after a viral infection. These infections include the common cold, sore throat, and stomach or intestinal viruses, with vomiting and diarrhea. The nerves are attacked, and the nerve insulation and sometimes even the covered conducting part of the nerve are damaged, and signals are delayed or otherwise changed. Abnormal sensations and weakness follow. Jimmy had had a virus the week before the symptoms began.

We had so much support from our family and friends. It was such a reminder of God's love to us as each one came in ready to do whatever needed to be done. They helped to see us through each day with conversation, laughter, and most importantly prayer.

Jimmy was in a small group of men called Promise Keepers, and they all came one night together and cut up with him and had a time of prayer around his bed. That meant so much to us. We were both so weary of the hospital and of the constant flow of traffic into the room.

God led me to **Job 33: 19-26 (NKJV): "Man is also chastened with pain on his bed, and with strong pain in many of his bones, so that his life abhors** bread and his soul succulent food. His flesh wastes away from sight, and his bones stick out which once were not seen. Yes, his soul draws near the pit, and his life to the executioners. If there is a messenger for him, a mediator, one among a thousand, to show man His uprightness, then He is gracious to him, and says deliver him from going down to the pit; I have found a ransom; His flesh shall be young like a child's. He shall pray to God, and He will delight in him, He shall see His face with joy, for He restores to man His righteousness."

In the Living Bible what really stood out to me was **verse 26b, "and he will return to his duties."** I knew God was telling me Jimmy would be alright and return to his job at some point. What comfort and peace that gave me as I continued to draw from this Word which sustained me during the months to come.

Jimmy literally could not swallow at one point and had to have a feeding tube placed in his stomach to give him medicine and nourishment. I witnessed the word God had given me come true as Jimmy lost weight and muscle tone and his bones stuck out.

My husband had been in the credit union business thirty plus years, ever since his Army duties were over. We received unbelievable support from these fine folks. One larger credit union actually sent one of their employees to manage the credit union at little cost, and a group of guys were volunteering to drive Jimmy to work every day whenever he was able to return to work. We were simply amazed at the generosity extended to us and will never forget all the people involved.

Staying in God's Word was my greatest source of strength and He gave me many words of promise that He was with me as indicated in the following verses:

Isaiah 43: 1-3a (NKJV),

"But now, thus says the Lord, who created you, O Jacob,
and He who formed you, O Israel:
'Fear not, for I have redeemed you;
I have called you by your name;
you are mine.
When you pass through the waters, I will be with you;
and through the rivers, they shall not overflow you,
When you walk through the fire, you shall not be burned,
nor shall the flame scorch you."

Daniel 10: 12 (NKJV) says, **"Then he said to me, 'Do not fear, Daniel (Sandra), for from the first day that you set your heart to understand, and to humble yourself before your God, your words were heard; and I have come because of your words.' For I am the Lord your God, The Holy One of Israel, your Savior."**

Isaiah 48:10b (KJV), "Behold, I have refined thee, but not with silver; I have chosen you in the furnace of affliction." My dear friend, Joan once told me that our family was chosen. I said, "yes, chosen in affliction." I never fully understood the whole meaning of that, but affliction has been a constant companion for us in one way or another it seems! I must have needed a lot of refining! I remember asking my Dad why everything had to be so hard and seemingly tragic.

Another passage I clung to during this time was **Job 23: 10 (NIV), "But He knows the way that I take; when He has tested me; I shall come forth as gold."** I pray we will past His test.

Someone asked me if I was afraid. How could I be afraid with the words of promise God gave me each day? Confirmation of His presence with us and His promise of restoration was all I needed. You see Guillian-Barre reacts so differently with folks, so I knew Jimmy might end up on a respirator if the disease progressed into his diaphragm. He came very close at one point but praise God he didn't have to.

I believe that our prayers and those others offered across the state were heard by God and that He healed Jimmy to bring Himself the greater glory through it all. In fact, today Jimmy is at least 95% restored. He has very few limitations in bodily movement. Many others who suffer continue to have certain limitations. We even know of a young man that recently passed away due to complications from the disease.

God once again gave me His Word in **Isaiah 35:3-4 (NKJV)**, which reads, **"Strengthen the weak hands, and make firm the feeble knees. Say to those who are fearful-hearted, 'Be strong, do not fear! Behold, your God will come with vengeance, with the recompense of God; He will come and save you.' "**

God has allowed us to minister to other couples because of our afflictions, which we hope brought them peace and hope, as their loved one lay unable to move. It was encouraging for them to see Jimmy walk in to visit. We were able to share our faith and trust in our Lord with them.

For the first time we knew what being handicapped meant. Our experience deepened our appreciation for those persons with disabilities and for their caretakers. Our short period of affliction was nothing compared to the lifetime care given by many folks to their loved ones. I have prayed often for God to give physical and emotional strength to caregivers because of our experience.

We met many wonderful people through this trial, including the doctors, nurses, and therapists. Many have remained very special to us, and we stay in contact to this day. A nurse asked us one day when we returned for a visit how we kept from becoming angry and bitter. We were able to explain the peace of God through the process and the knowledge that He was in control.

A psychiatrist came to see Jimmy one day while he was in the hospital, and left saying, "I will not be back because I can see your faith is seeing you through." What an opportunity to show the peace that only God can give! Many don't understand that kind of peace that passes all human understanding. The tests we are going through allow us to be a witness of Christ's goodness and faithfulness. People see something in us that they desire to have, and it opens doors to share the Gospel and our hope we have in Christ.

In Isaiah 60: 1-3 (NKJV) it says,
"Arise, shine; for your light has come!
And the glory of the Lord is risen upon you.
For behold, the darkness shall cover the earth,
and deep darkness the people;
but the Lord will arise over you,
and His glory will be seen upon you.
The Gentiles shall come to your light,
and kings to the brightness of your rising."

Oh, this is my prayer, that I will arise and shine in whatever circumstance I find myself and that I will be a bold and faithful witness always ready to share the hope in me with a dark and lost world. I desire His glory to be seen upon me, so that one day I will hear those awesome words, "Well, done my good and faithful servant, you have been faithful over little, now I will make you ruler over much."

Can you imagine the glory that shown forth from Moses as he came down off that mountain, having been with the Lord? As he completely rested and intimately fellowshipped with the Lord those many days, Moses radiated as he came down the mountain amongst his people. By staying close to the Lord in His Word, through prayer, and through Bible study, others will be able to see Jesus in us. We may be the only Jesus they ever see. All we experience in our lives as we live for Him is for His glory and for our eternal reward in heaven.

Does that convict you? It does me. Oh Lord, help my wrong attitudes, words, and actions.

Psalm 139: 23-24 (AMP) states, **"Search me [thoroughly], O God, and know my heart; try me and know my thoughts. And see if there is any wicked or hurtful way in me, and lead me in the way everlasting."** As I began to pray this passage years ago, God took me at my word and began to show me all the wickedness in my heart. Unforgiveness, anger, pride, and selfishness He has drawn out. Is He through working on me? Not a chance. The work will continue throughout my life on earth.

> *Prayer: Father, we thank You for walking with us through yet another journey. Thank You for the healing and the strength to get through each new day with a sense of humor and peace. Thank You for how we have been privileged to minister to other families struggling with the same diagnosis in their lives. We pray You will minister to their hearts and draw them closer to You, Amen.*

CHAPTER TEN

God Sent the Locust to Strip Us

I reflected on a journal entry from **Joel 2:25-27 (NKJV), "So I will restore to you the years that the swarming locust has eaten, the crawling locust, the consuming locust, And the chewing locust, my great army which I sent among you. You shall eat in plenty and be satisfied, and praise the name of the LORD your God, Who has dealt wondrously with you; and My people shall never be put to shame. Then you shall know that I am in the midst of Israel: I am the LORD your God and there is no other. My people shall never be put to shame."**

I had never thought of the fact that maybe God sent the locusts for a season in my life to accomplish His purposes in me. The locust moved in and completely ate away everything in their path. Is God stripping me? Maybe we are too quick to blame everything on the devil. Did God send the locust to strip you?

We must realize that whatever Satan does is filtered through the Father's hands. He works all things together for our good. **"And we know that all things work together for good to those who love God, to those who are the called according to his purpose." Romans 8:28 (NKJV).** God teaches me more each day that He is working all things together for my good and His glory.

I continue to be concerned over Robbie as he appears to have no spiritual desire to follow God's direction for his life. God led me to **Isaiah 14:24 (AMP), "Surely, as I have thought and planned, so shall it come to pass, and as I have purposed, so shall it stand."**

Jeremiah 1:5a (NIV) states, "Before I formed you in the womb I knew you; before you were born I set you apart;" I thank God for His encouragement to me in regards to our son. I have told Rob many times that God has a purpose for his life if he will stop running and allow the Lord to work. I thank God for His encouragement to me through His Word in regards to our son.

I sometimes feel much like the psalmist in **Psalm 77** over the issues with Robbie. **Verse 3 (KJV)** says, **"I remembered God, and was troubled; I complained, and my spirit was overwhelmed."** In **verse 6, "I call to remembrance my song in the night; I meditate within my heart, and my spirit makes diligent search."**

David was remembering a time when things were better in his life and when life was good. He felt downhearted, maybe even wondered where God was in all that was happening. Do you ever feel like that? Do you wonder where God is and if He really cares about your concerns? Haven't we all at one time or another?

I am always reminded of the passages that tell me He will never leave me nor forsake me. Those words are comforting to me, and I pray they are to you in your time of grief and despair. I recall as the psalmist did the days when the Lord protected and kept me in his grasp through earlier days.

I must keep my focus on my Father who is named Immanuel, God with us. He is the great "I AM". **Matthew 1:23 (NAS) reads, "Behold, the virgin shall be with child, and shall bear a Son, and they shall call His name Immanuel."** which is translated, **"God with us."** Praise the Lord! What would we do without His presence?

I saw a note in the church bulletin to join a group of ladies in prayer on Sunday mornings (which I have referred to in previous chapters), and was convicted to attend the following Sunday. Joan, who leads the time, told me that it had been an accident that it was announced. It was no accident to me, but out of almost five thousand members, I was the only one who came to pray that Sunday. I knew God had drawn me to that group for His purposes. We pray for the church body, the pastors, and the leadership. We pray scripture back to the Father. This is a new experience for me. I am learning so much, even in my seventh year.

We might read a Word that Joan, our leader, receives from the Lord, and then pray it as we felt the Lord led us to do. Sometimes we have scriptures the Lord lays on our individual hearts during the week, and we pray those back to Him.

I really am developing a hunger and thirst for the Word of God. **"As the deer pants for the water brooks, so pants my soul for You, O God. My soul thirsts for God, for the living God." Psalm 42:1-2a (NAS)** reads. God speaks specifically through His Word to the circumstances in my life. It is very exciting and encouraging applying what was written years ago to my current situation.

"But his delight is in the law of the LORD, and in His law he meditates day and night," says David in **Psalm 1:2 (NKJV)**. This is where I often found myself day and night, seeking the Lord with all my heart and soul. I was praying for my son and family every moment I could. I spent time diligently searching the scripture for any Word He would have for me.

This was when I began to discover that God's Word was alive and active. Whatever I was going through the Lord would lead me to an encouraging passage, and then I would be able to walk in faith that He was working, not only in Robbie, but in me. Sometimes I did not want to hear what He was telling me but I learned to trust Him and recognize His voice through His Word, His messenger, a song, my circumstances, and through prayer.

I am beginning to learn some ways I have given the devil a foothold in my life, and I am getting rid of objects I have allowed in my home through ignorance. I am getting rid of certain reading materials and music and anything else the Lord leads me to. I am committing to fast from fictional reading in order to dwell in His Word and keep my mind stayed on Him.

The Lord reminds me of a voodoo doll that was given to us as a gag gift on Jimmy's 40th birthday as a joke. I recall right where it is and I decide to discard it. It is interesting that I had thought the gift was so funny when given to him at the time.

Spiritual warfare is so real. We should be knowledgeable about the wiles of the devil. The scriptures that come to mind in this regard include **Hosea 4:6 (NKJV), "My people are destroyed for lack of knowledge,"** and **II Corinthians 2:11 (NKJV), "Lest Satan should take advantage of us; for we are not ignorant of his devices."** Whether or not we realize it, when we enter into the kingdom of God through our salvation experience, we become the enemy of Satan.

God's Word tells us in James 4:7-10 (NKJV), "Therefore submit to God. Resist the devil, and he will flee from you. Draw near to God, and He will draw near to you. Cleanse your hands, you sinners; and purify your hearts, you double-minded. Lament and mourn and weep! Let your laughter be turned to mourning and your joy to gloom. Humble yourselves in the sight of the Lord, and He will lift you up." If we are to submit to God we will come up under His commandments, obey Him and follow His leading in our lives.

To resist the devil means to take your stand against. We cannot straddle the fence in our alliance to the Father; either we are for Him or against Him. We cannot have one foot in both territories. That is when He tells us we are lukewarm in our faith, and He wants to spew us out. I can understand that because I dislike lukewarm coffee. I want it to be piping hot when I drink it. In like manner, I want to be on fire for my Lord in all I do or say. I don't want to be spewed out!

We tend to put God on the back burner of our lives with just enough heat to keep it simmering. I want to be boiling! I want the passion of my life to be about my Abba Father and to come down from my mountain time with Him showing forth the glory of God, so that all who see me will know I have been with my Father. I fail so miserably in that, but that is my heart's desire. He is still working to make me holy unto Him and will till the day I die.

We are to draw near to the Lord with intimate fellowship. Our relationship requires more from us than just a salvation experience. He wants to grow us and develop our lives to be used for his glory on this earth and in preparation for eternity. Oh that we would all understand that fact!

I have a great example of what my Heavenly Father is like through the example of my earthly father. He walks closely with the Lord and seeks His direction which has not always been popular with others, but he always remains steadfast. I remember seeing my Dad pulling aside to have his quiet time with his Lord and seeing his head bowed in prayer so often. He was and is my spiritual example on earth and has taught me to love the Lord in ways he will never know, just by his daily example.

I am learning that the enemy can pollute a place with his unholy presence. At this point, the place or maybe a person may need to be prayed over and sometimes even anointed with the oil of the Holy Spirit. Any ground given to the enemy even through ignorance needs to be taken back in the powerful name of the Living Lord Jesus Christ.

In His Word, the Amplified Bible says in **Luke 1:20 (AMP), "And lo, you will be and will continue to be silent, and not able to speak till the day when these things take place, because you have not believed what I told you; but my words are of a kind which will be fulfilled in the appointed and proper time."** Forgive me, Lord, for my unbelief. I do know things will come together in Your appointed and proper time. The Holy Spirit reminds me of the passage in **Luke 1:37, "For with God nothing is ever impossible, and no word from God shall be without power or impossible of fulfillment."**

I admit I am having trouble believing that God is going to work through my circumstances for my good and His glory. I just want it to be now. Like most Americans, I have trouble waiting. In our modern day we don't have to wait for much with fast food, microwaves, and supersonic transportation. We seek instant gratification, but I realize that God is doing a work that will be done "in the appointed and proper time".

I am reminded of a friend's friend who told her with regards to her son's situation, "Stand back and let him work out his own testimony." That is so hard to do as a parent because we don't want our children to make mistakes or to suffer the consequences of their mistakes, yet they must.

I am learning that the enemy desires our children for his service and that he does all he can to entice them into sin and tries to defile their minds and bodies through what they listen to and watch. He is the prince of the air and has certainly influenced the world with his devices. I am also learning that, "Greater is He who is in me than he that is in the world." God is calling us to stand in the gap for our loved ones through prayer.

In **Joshua 8:18 and 26 (NIV)," Then the LORD said to Joshua, 'Hold out toward Ai the javelin that is in your hand, for into your hand I will deliver the city.' So Joshua held out his javelin toward Ai.... For Joshua did not draw back the hand that held out his javelin until he had destroyed all who lived in Ai. But Israel did carry off for themselves the livestock and plunder of this city, as the LORD had instructed Joshua."**

In a powerful little book given to me years ago entitled, <u>The Conquest of Canaan</u> by Jessie Penn-Lewis, it says:

> "All that Joshua did was to stretch his hand out, and KEEP IT OUT until the entire city was taken. Notice here the combination of faith and action. The warriors had to engage in actual fighting, but Joshua had to take the faith-position of *keeping his hand stretched out.* How strange these ways of gaining victory in the Old Testament! Moses on the hillside lifting his hands, and now Joshua stretching out his hand

while Israel went forward to take the city. Elisha, in his day, told the king to strike an arrow on the ground, and when he struck three times he told him he had settled the limit of his victory, and would get victory three times and no more. These pictures of faith and action are very remarkable and seem to show the leaders and prophets as DEALING WITH THE INVISIBLE FORCES, while the rank and file went to the actual war.

The power over the invisible forces of evil lies in the ATTITUDE OF FAITH, and if you are not able to go down to the battlefield, you can in your own room take the attitude of victory, stretching out the javelin by faith for others in the front of the battle with sin and Satan.....

....You can thus take the attitude in your will, simply saying, 'I stand with God for victory there, and there, and there,' and quietly settle down to hold it, until the ground is taken for the Lord. There must not be a looking at appearances or difficulties but a tenacious faith that the invisible principalities and powers must give way before the believer stretching out by faith the "javelin", thus indicating the conquering, overmastering power of God."[1]

So we must take the javelin of faith, believing that God loves us and is more concerned for our children then we are. Even when we can't be out on the battlefield with them we can be at home or wherever we are in intercession for them, as the Lord fights the battle for their very souls. We must never give up, but continue to stand on the promises of our Lord. Even when we don't see His hand in our situation, we must trust His plan. I am not saying it is easy. Believe me, I am still in shallow waters, but I pray that He will take me deeper and deeper with Him in my journey of faith.

> *Prayer: Thank you Lord for teaching me Your truths. Thank you that you have provided a way for us to come into Your very chambers in intimate relationship with You. Thank You that we can claim victory in You as we take on the attitude of faith, knowing that You are fighting our battles. Praise to our Commander-in-Chief, Amen.*

CHAPTER ELEVEN

Standing in the Gap

"And I sought for a man among them who should build up a wall, and stand in the gap before Me for the land, that I should not destroy it, but I found none!" Ezekiel 22:30, (Amp).

I have found that my walk with the Lord will not always be easy, but if I keep my eyes on Jesus He will see me through. I have some scriptures jotted down from another season of winter; a low period in my life that I hope will encourage you as you walk through your trials and struggles.

Psalm 27: 8-9 (NKJV), "When You said, 'Seek my face', my heart said to You, 'Your face, Lord, I will seek.' Do not hide Your face from me; do not turn Your servant away in anger; You have been my help; do not leave me nor forsake me, O God of my salvation." To me, when it says seek God's face, it means to seek His presence, His nearness, and when you do you can literally feel His arms around you. You have to come to a point when you desire Him more than anything this world has to offer.

II Chronicles 15:2b (NKJV), The Lord is with you while you are with Him. If you seek Him, He will be found by you; but if you forsake Him, He will forsake you."

II Chronicles 16:9 (NKJV), "For the eyes of the Lord run to and fro, throughout the whole earth, to show Himself strong on behalf of those whose heart is loyal to Him."

I attempt to seek after Him at all times, not just because I have to but, because I want to. I listen to messages and Christian songs, read the Word daily, and participate in Bible Study whether in a group or on my own. I meditate on scriptures I have in a separate journal that have meant so much to my life at a particular time and place.

My husband, Jimmy, has recently lost his job, and I am seeing some old signs in Robbie that reveal that he is returning to the way of the world once again. He denies the use of drugs, but he is staying out late, and the anger and mood swings have become evident as in days past. So we continue to be surrounded with difficulties. Some are because of the choices other individuals have made.

I called Robbie's probation officer to ask him to check him for drugs and to come down hard on him. Sure enough he tested positive. He has had a heartbreaking breakup with his girlfriend, and even though I know that was of God, it is a loss that is very painful to him. I can tell Rob is searching once again for the quick fix to fill the void in his heart. Only God can do that as I have shared with him so many times.

Oh Lord, are we headed back down the same path of destruction? We, as his family, see the signs and attempt to warn him of impending consequences of going back to the old way of life, but he resists over and over again.

We warned him that he is headed to prison again, but he either does not believe it or does not care. He began to stay out all night and disappeared for weeks at a time without contact. When we do have contact it, is not pleasant. He is shutting his family out, even his daughters at this point. Christmas Day was a disaster as he came to see the girls open their gifts. He might as well not have been there because he wasn't in the right spirit or frame of mind. He was unkempt and slept most of the time. He came to the table, but would not eat with the rest of the family and ended up leaving angry as we tried to draw him back in. Later he told me he was so ashamed and could only think of going to get his next hit. Oh, the enemy has enticed him back into his snare.

I am reminded of an incident I saw the other day in my own yard. As I looked out my kitchen window at the area where I have a birdfeeder, I saw a cat crouched down. He was part Siamese, so I was admiring him because I have had several Siamese cats and always liked the breed.

I got my coffee and went over to have my quiet time before work. Suddenly I was startled to hear the distressing cry of a bird. As I went back to that same window I saw the cat with a bird in its mouth taking off across the yard looking back every once in a while to see if anything was following. A larger bird, I assumed the Mother, was swooping down trying to get him to turn loose of the baby bird. I know it is the way nature works, but it was disturbing to me, and I wanted to go chase the cat and get the bird away from its clutches.

What a terrifying picture of the enemy, Satan, who goes about the earth seeking whom he may devour! He appears so attractive and harmless and then waits for his opportunity to take his victim into his clutches and devour them. Oh, that we would be alert to his tactics. He is certainly using the drug scene to destroy those addicted to it and their families. I pray each day for their freedom from his clutches.

As a Mother, I am determined to stand in the gap for my son's very soul, and I will never give up crying out to the Lord for his very life. There is a poem by an unknown author that I would like to share with anyone who finds themselves standing in the gap for a loved one.

Standing in the Gap

"I'll stand in the gap for my son
I'll stand till the victory is won
This one thing I know that You love him so,
And Your work in my son is not done
I'll stand in the gap everyday and there I will fervently pray,
And Lord, don't let me waver
If things get quite rough, which they may,
I'll never give up on that boy.
Nor will You, for You promised him joy,
For I know that it's true when he said yes to You,
Though the enemy seeks to destroy
I'll not quit as I intercede for you are his Savior indeed.
Though it may take years
I give You my fears as I trust every moment I plead
And so in the gap I will stand
Heeding your every command
With help from above I'll unconditionally love,
And soon he will reach for your hand!" (1)

Let's review this chapters leading verse. **Ezekiel 22:30 (AMP)** says, **"And I sought for a man among them who should build up the wall, and stand in the gap before Me for the land, that I should not destroy it, but I found none."**

Will you be found standing in the gap for your loved one? It is hard work but oh so worth it!

I have an electric candle burning in one window, not because I am waiting for my son to come home from the war, but so he will see it as he passes by some night and know it as a welcome home sign. It is actually a spiritual battle we as families fight as we continue to stand in the gap for our prodigals. He calls us to be the light in the darkness.

> *Prayer: Lord, I promise to stand in the gap for our son, never giving up until we see him coming home from the land of the enemy. We believe Your promise to one day bring Him home to Your dear self. Lord, we pray You will do whatever it takes! Do the work in me You need to do in order to make me into a vessel You can use. One day I hope to see him return to You, Amen.*

CHAPTER TWELVE

Our Prodigal's Continued Rebellion

"He let Himself be regarded as a criminal and be numbered with the transgressors, yet He bore [and took away] the sin of many and makes intercession for the transgressors—the rebellious." Isaiah 53:12b, (AMP).

It is the beginning of a new year, and I wonder what it holds for us. I am claiming **I Peter 2:25 (NIV)** for Robbie. **"For you were like sheep going astray, but have now returned to the Shepherd and Overseer of your souls."** The sheep which returns is hopefully my son coming back from enemy territory, fully repentant. I pray that will happen in his life this year. I look up at the picture in my office of the Shepherd reaching over the cliff to pull the lost and injured lamb into His bosom. It is such a picture of what His love does for us all and for my son.

Christ goes after the one who is lost. In **Ezekiel 34:11-16 (NKJV), "For thus says the Lord God: 'Indeed I Myself will search for My sheep and seek them out. As a shepherd seeks out his flock on the day he is among his scattered sheep, so will I seek out My sheep and deliver them from all the places where they were scattered on a cloudy and dark day. And I will bring them out from the peoples and gather them from the countries, and I will bring them to their own land; I will feed them on the mountains of Israel, in the valleys and in all the inhabited places of the country. I will feed them in good pasture, and their fold shall be on the high mountains of Israel. There** they shall lie down in a good fold and feed in rich pasture on the mountains of Israel. I will feed My flock, and I will make them lie down,' says the Lord God. 'I will seek what was lost and bring back what was driven away, bind up the broken and strengthen what was sick; but I will destroy the fat and the strong, and feed them in judgment." This is a promise of regathering and restoration.

I am reminded of the little prayer group of mother's I told you about who used to meet in our home years ago to pray for our prodigals and how the Lord had given us the passage about the Shepherd leaving the ninety-nine and going after the lost sheep who had wandered away from his watch.

Isaiah 53:12b says, ".....Yet he bore [and took away] the sin of many and makes intercession for the transgressors—the rebellious." Thank you, Lord. It gives me such comfort to know You are praying for Robbie.

Have you ever been rebellious in your walk with the Lord? We are all prodigals at one time or another in our lives if we would admit it. Walking in our own way is disobedience to God's perfect will for our lives.

We had to confront Robbie with some issues once again, and he denies his involvement. I find myself asking our son to leave our home this time. He will not abide by the rules and continues to do his own thing. He packed his clothes commenting that he doesn't have anywhere to go. It breaks my heart, but we cannot allow his rebellious lifestyle to continue. If he wants to destroy his life, he will have to do it somewhere else. It hurts too much seeing him make so many wrong choices. I weep as he prepares to leave once again and the same vice is squeezing my heart.

I turned to **Psalm 46:1-2a, 10a (NKJV)** in my quiet time. The Lord's message for me was, **"God is our refuge and strength, a very present help in trouble. We will not fear. Be still and know that I am God."** I am learning more and more to give Robbie over to God. Little by little I am finding strength to release him. I still keep trying to take things back into my control, but God is teaching me.

Some days I am so weary from life's battles. What encouragement I read in **Isaiah 40:28-31 (NKJV), "Have you not known? Have you not heard? The everlasting God, the LORD, the Creator of the ends of the earth, neither faints nor is weary. His understanding is unsearchable. He gives power to the weak, and to those who have no might He increases strength. Even the youths shall faint and be weary, and the young men shall utterly fall, but those who wait on the LORD Shall renew their strength; they shall mount up with wings like eagles, They shall run and not be weary, They shall walk and not faint."**

I cannot keep up with what he is doing all the time but I know the all seeing God, El Roi, can. There is no place Robbie can run that he can escape the eye of the Lord. He might be able to escape our eye but not the Lord's.

A friend saw Robbie at the car wash where he is working and said he looks pale and miserable. The Lord allows us to hear about him occasionally and at least to know he is alive. God is giving me total peace at this point of our journey.

Robbie called wanting money, but I told him no. He got real angry and told me to have a great life and the phone line was dead. God immediately took me to **Nehemiah 4:14b (NKJV), "Do not be afraid of them. Remember the Lord, great and awesome, and fight for your brethren, your sons, your daughters, your wives, and your houses."** I continue to fight for my children and my household as I intercede on their behalf.

I received a newsletter written by Jack Hayford that really spoke to me and I wanted to share it with you because it gave me much encouragement and I pray it will you if you have a prodigal.

> "Whispers in the Wind," calling children home. Every March brings the reminder of God's dealing with young people to establish His will in their lives. This March, He is ready to do the same.
>
> In Isaiah 43:5-7, God declares His commitment to breathe His call to our descendents "from the west, the north and the south. He says, "I will bring them, I will say, Give them up. Do not keep them back. Believe my Word of promise. There is no place My voice cannot reach your children. Call unto Me---and I will call unto them!
>
> In response: Let me pray with you. "Heavenly Father, my heart is touched with gratitude to remember, how you kept me and brought me to obedience and submission to Your will. Now I stand with fellow servants who lift their hands to receive your promise.
>
> Bring the children home Lord! Jesus said, **"The wind blows where it wishes, and you hear the sound of it, but cannot tell where it comes from and where it goes. So is everyone who is born of the Spirit". John 3:8 (NKJV).**

With those words our Lord not only describes God's supernatural ability to breathe life into deadened spirits, but also He teaches us the wisdom of refusing to doubt He is at work in people we despair of reaching or in human circumstances we think may be beyond redemption

Even now, I am already going before you, faithful servant. I am breathing into the dark corners of hearts that are darkened, blinded, bound and tormented. Though no one knows what I am doing or with whom I am dealing each one of them is aware of it!"[1]

Wow, what encouragement that gives to anyone who is praying for a prodigal. Praise God He is dealing with them.

Robbie has met a girl named Tina at work and is apparently staying with her at her grandmother's house. I do not like it at all, and it seems his rebellion goes on and on. He is living a lifestyle that defies all we have taught him.

Prayer: Thank You Lord for interceding on behalf of Your lost sheep. It gives me such encouragement to know that You go after the lost sheep and bind up the wounded, Amen.

CHAPTER THIRTEEN

Evilness Versus Foolishness

"Set a guard over my mouth, O Lord. Keep watch over the door of my mouth. Let not my heart be drawn to what is evil, to take part in wicked deeds with men who are evildoers; let me not eat of their delicacies. Keep me from the snares they have laid for me, from the traps set by evildoers. Let the wicked fall into their own nets, while I pass by in safety." Psalm 141:3 (NIV).

I pray that my children will make God the top priority in their lives. I pray they will develop their own intimate relationship with the Father and know His peace. He is worthy to be praised and adored. God continues to give me the promise of restoration from where the locusts came and stripped us. I keep looking forward to that day but know that much work still needs to be accomplished in all of us still.

In **Hebrews 6:15 (NIV) it says, "And so after waiting patiently Abraham received what was promised."** We may endure a time of testing and patience as we wait on Him to fulfill His promises. What He promises He will do because He is not a God who lies.

Remember Isaiah 55:8-9 that points out how God's plans are not our plans and His thoughts are not our thoughts? Isn't that the truth! So many times we can't foresee that our plan would have brought disaster to our lives, but God's plan was so much better. He is Sovereign. He knows all and sees all and is working for us a perfect plan. Why do we kick and fight against it so many times in our lives? Human nature!

I am praying this for Robbie now, "**Set a guard over [his] mouth, O Lord. Keep watch over the door of [his] mouth. Let not [his] heart be drawn to what is evil, to take part in wicked deeds with men who are evildoers; let [him] not eat of their delicacies. Keep [him] from the snares they have laid for [him], from the traps set by evildoers. Let the wicked fall into their own nets, while [he] passes by in safety." Psalm 141:3 (NIV).**

It is interesting that I received a letter from Robbie a few days later telling me about the wicked people he saw every day. The Lord had led me to pray for him to be kept from evildoers and this was confirmation that I was on the right track in my prayers for him.

In a book I am reading it makes the distinction between an evil person and a foolish person. It might be helpful to identify what you are dealing with in your prodigal. It is entitled <u>Bold Love</u> by Dr. Dan B. Allender & Dr. Tremper Longman III. The following comes from this book:

> "Evil is present when there is a profound absence of empathy, shame, and goodness. Empathy involves a connectedness to the heart of another and a respect for their personal boundaries. An evil person is unmoved by the inner world of the other and has no respect for boundaries. Shame involves an ability to be exposed and disturbed about actual or perceived violations of relationships. An evil person is unaffected by exposure, so is consequently shameless. Finally, goodness involves a desire to see someone or something grow in strength, freedom, and beauty. An evil person seems to delight in stripping away purpose, individuality, and vitality.
>
> Evil is (for the most part) unfeeling. It lacks sorrow when someone suffers and joy when there is happiness. But an evil person is more than emotionally detached; he simply will not allow himself to enter the heart of his victim as a person.....
>
> Evil is devoid of conscience. It lacks moral boundaries; right is whatever it desires. A seared conscience does not respond with mercy to a cry for help, nor is it stopped by the threat of shame......

Evil uses arrogance and mockery to escape being shamed. The ability to cover loneliness and fear of rejection without reliance on the mercy of God is predicated on a hardening of the soul through arrogance and a blinding of the eyes through mockery (Proverbs 21:24). Mockery may take obvious forms, such as biting sarcasm and vicious cynicism, or it can be much more subtle.......

Fools on the other hand are said to live for little more than the moment. A fool's hot anger (directed at self or others), self-centeredness, and hatred of discipline and wisdom are not essentially different from the qualities that line the heart of an evil person, but there is a difference in degree. Sin is essentially the same in the saint as in the reprobate. The most godly men and women I know still struggle with petty anger, jealousy, selfishness, and ambivalence toward wisdom. Nevertheless, they are lovers of wisdom and imbued with a fragrant scent of heaven. At first blush, one can say we all struggle with sin; therefore, the one inclined to evil and the one who hungers after wisdom with regard to the capacity to do harm are much more alike than different. On the other hand, with regard to living out truth and love, they are different enough to warrant notice.

In many respects, an evil person is simply a more severe fool who has progressed to a level of foolishness that is deeply severed from human emotion (empathy and shame) and human involvement (devouring destruction). An evil person is a more crafty and deceitful fool who is more artful at destructive thrill of controlling and then consuming his victim. The points of similarity and difference may help further clarify each category.....

Although an evil person does not feel the pain of another, he is highly perceptive and often a master of predicting other people's shame, fear, and loneliness. Evil does not truly feel and devouring. An evil person's anger is cold-blooded and merely a prelude to stunning his victims in order to draw closes enough to swallow them up.

A fool, on the other hand, is not usually cold and unfeeling. In fact, he may be very warm and sympathetic, but not for long. His feelings are usually like a travelogue instead of a real trip. They are a brief emotional excursion that hits the highlights, but never ventures into the smells and sounds that make up a real city. Once real depth of feeling and relationship is required, the fool is usually bored or distracted to other matters that are more personally rewarding. The fool, unlike the one inclined to evil, feels connected to the inner world of others, but only to the degree that it requires little of him. Once something is required, the fool will deaden his own inner world and cut off the connection with the other through anger.

A fool's anger is often intimidating and intense. Overt behavior can be misleading, however, because evil can be explosive and foolishness can appear calm. It takes a wise heart to discern the motivational energy behind appearances. The evil person is like a black widow who frightens, turns, and traps her victim with the intention of moving in closer to do more harm. The fool is more like a grizzly bear whose primary goal is to intimidate and frighten in order to establish his preeminence and independence, and gain compliance and control. Evil wants to enslave and destroy; foolishness desires to be adored and obeyed. A fool's anger is disproportionate to the situation, impulsive, and repetitive.....

The fool lacks self-control and is reckless (Proverbs 12:23, 14:16, 20:3, 29:20). Not only is the fool a thunderous storm, but the storm is also one that can develop suddenly out of a clear, sunny day. Most people find such storm fronts utterly intimidating, to a point that they are too frightened to wander out in the open terrain, not knowing when and if lightning will strike......

Impulsivity is a means of acting without bearing responsibility for an act. We seem to live with the presumption that if we did not do something with calculating intentionality, then we cannot be held as responsible. Impulsivity is a decoy, a cover-up of the deeper commitment to find satisfaction, irrespective of the consequences to self or others. Impulsivity is seldom a one-shot experience. Oddly, the activity of erratic, unpredictable, rash behavior is a pattern that can be predicted over time like clockwork. The fool regularly repeats his folly.

The classic proverb establishes a key element in the personality of the fool: 'As a dog returns to its vomit, so a fool repeats his folly' (Proverbs 26:11). It is a disgusting simile. A fool falls on his knees to lap up the vile substance of his foolishness and does so again and again. A fool compulsively returns to what has worked to keep shame and loneliness at a distance.

Anger is effective in keeping people at bay and the inner ache subdued. Anger is used to intimidate ('Stay away, I don't want you close enough to see me and provoke shame'). It is also used to demand ('Don't go too far away, I don't want you to leave me and provoke loneliness'). Anger, like a thick wall, keeps alien, unwanted inner realities outside awareness. The fool uses anger to demand that nothing inhibits him from being on the center stage of life. His rage is utterly self-centered......

The heart of the fool is empty, but it feels full because it finds satisfaction in the transitory and material world. When the fool says, 'There is no God' (Psalm 14:1, 53:1), he is not saying that God does not exist, but that God does not matter. What does matter is what he can lay his hands on to fill his soul......

A fool is insatiable but easily pleased. The sentence may appear to be contradictory, but there is an odd logic to the point. A fool lives to fill his belly, but the only true fullness comes from humble dependence on the mercy of God. The fool sees God as an interloper who meddles in the rightful business of life. Consequently, the fool either ignores God or compartmentalizes God and then sanitizes Him to be as he desires. Dealing with God in this way leaves an untouched emptiness in the fool's heart that can never be filled as long as he lives in rebellion. The fool will always be insatiable, always looking for more to fill the emptiness, and even more, to numb the awareness of his hatred of God.

Yet the choice to ignore God makes temporary satisfaction much more fulfilling. I have always been amazed that fools seem to be happier than those who are wise. One reason is that the fool has options available for happiness that those who seek wisdom know will only deepen shame and sorrow, and will harm those they love. At the time, I am less than thrilled with the options of holiness. I'd prefer a denial-based, hedonistic holiday like Mardi Gras to the pew-sitting solemnity of a Christmas Eve children's pageant. The fool can sate his appetite on folly without bearing much of an inner battle of shame. I am sad to say that at times I envy him, until I see his demise (Psalm 73).

What seems to thrill the soul of the fool more than drugs, sex, food, or any other quick-filling addiction is the sound of his own voice. I have met recovering alcoholics, sexaholics, bulimics, Christians of all stripes, pastors, counselors, Indian chiefs, and CEOs who were transported by the sound of their own intoxicating babble. They were no longer as enslaved by their primary addiction, but they were still addicted to the presumption that they had the steps to life and the know how to lead everyone to the new Promised Land. Nothing is more difficult to bear than a bore or a person who 'delights in airing his own opinions' (Proverbs 18:2). The fool thinks he's right in everything he does (Proverbs 12:15), whether it's interpreting a Bible passage or operating a sewing machine. The fool is easily filled, especially with his own grandiosity, but he is blind to the consequences of his direction in life.......

The fool believes there is an answer to the emptiness that only heaven can fill. Consequently, he will give his heart of whatever activity or substance seems to provide relief from the dull internal ache. The fool seems to be an expert at calculating gain, but is unable to look deeply at the inevitability of loss.

The fool is so self-centered and self-reliant that he is deaf, dumb, and blind to the consequences of his choices. He will follow a path that seems to be right, even when the blacktop gives way to gravel and gravel to dirt and dirt to rocks and debris. Almost nothing will stop the fool from plunging ahead into peril."

This really helped me in identifying what I was dealing with in Robbie's case. He has definitely got the characteristics of the fool in his life. He doesn't like discipline but faces it all the time due to his rebellion from other sources. God certainly has put a bite in the consequences, and he has had to endure them, but I wonder if it has taken hold yet. He must come in total repentance and ask for help, which up to this point he has refused.

I hope this will help you identify your loved one and give you better insight how to pray for them. God can change the heart of either one.

Prayer: Lord, help me to keep Robbie constantly lifted up to You. Work in his heart and life so he will see you working all around him to protect him and sanctify him. May Rob turn from his foolishness to the pursuit of Your holiness, Lord, Amen.

CHAPTER FOURTEEN

Facts about Marijuana and Cocaine

"For nothing is impossible with God." Luke 1:37 (NIV).

Once again Robbie is incarcerated. We visit him often, and he is looking much better now. He was way underweight at 139 pounds when first incarcerated, due to the effects of drugs. He tells us he has gained up to 170 pounds. The internet is so helpful in gathering information about many topics, so I wanted to share what I found on this supposedly harmless substance.

Here is the article on marijuana from the National Institute on Drug Abuse:

> "Marijuana is the most commonly used illicit drug in the U. S. A dry, shredded green/brown mix of flowers, stems, seeds, and leaves of the hemp plan Cannabis sativa, it usually is smoked as a cigarette (joint, nail) or in a pipe (bong).
>
> It also is smoked in blunts, which are cigars that have been emptied of tobacco and refilled with marijuana, often in combination with another drug. Use also might include mixing marijuana in food or brewing it as a tea. As a more concentrated, resinous form it is called hashish and,

as a sticky black liquid, hash oil. Marijuana smoke has a pungent and distinctive, usually sweet-and-sour odor. There are countless street terms for marijuana including pot, herb, weed, grass, widow, ganja, and hash, as well as terms derived from trademarked varieties of cannabis, such as, Northern Lights, Fruity Juice, Afghani, and a number of Skunk varieties.

The main active chemical in marijuana is THC (delta-9-tetrahydrocannabinol). The membranes of certain nerve cells in the brain contain protein receptors that bind to THC. Once securely in place THC kicks off a series of cellular reactions that ultimately lead to the high that users experience when they smoke marijuana.

There were an estimated 2.6 million new marijuana users in 2001. This number is similar to the numbers of new users each year since 1995, but above the number in 1990 (1.6 million). In 2002, over 14 million Americans age 12 and older used marijuana at least once in the month prior to being surveyed, and 12.2 percent of past year marijuana users used marijuana on 300 or more days in the past 12 months. This translates into 3.1 million people using marijuana on a daily or almost daily basis over a 12-month period....

Scientists have learned a great deal about how THC acts in the brain to produce its many effects. When someone smokes marijuana, THC rapidly passes from the lungs into the bloodstream, which carries the chemical to organs throughout the body, including the brain.

In the brain, THC connects to specific sites called cannabinoid receptors on nerve cells and influences the activity of those cells. Some brain areas have many cannabinoid receptors; others have few or none. Many cannabinoid receptors are found in the parts of the brain that influence pleasure, memory, thought, concentration, sensory and time perception, and coordinated movement.

The short term effects of marijuana can include problems with memory and learning; distorted perception; difficulty in thinking and problem solving; loss of coordination; and increased heart rate. Research findings of long-term marijuana use indicate some changes in the brain similar to those seen after long-term use of other

major drugs of abuse. For example, cannabinoid withdrawal in chronically exposed animals leads to an increase in the activation of the stress-response system and changes in the activity of nerve cells containing dopamine. Dopamine neurons are involved in the regulation of motivation and reward, and are directly or indirectly affected by all drugs of abuse.

One study has indicated that a user's risk of heart attack more than quadruples in the first hour after smoking marijuana. The researchers suggest that such an effect might occur from marijuana's effects on blood pressure and heart rate and reduced oxygen-carrying capacity of blood.

A study of 450 individuals found that people who smoke marijuana frequently but did not smoke tobacco have more health problems and miss more days of work than nonsmokers.

Even infrequent use can cause burning and stinging of the mouth and throat, often accompanied by a heavy cough. Someone who smokes marijuana regularly may have many of the same respiratory problems that tobacco smokers do, such as daily cough and phlegm production, more frequent acute chest illness, a heightened risk of lung infections, and a greater tendency to obstructed airways . Smoking marijuana increases the likelihood of developing cancer of the head or neck, and the more marijuana smoked the greater the increase......

Depression, anxiety, and personality disturbances have been associated with marijuana use. Research clearly demonstrates that marijuana has potential to cause problems in daily life or make a person's existing problems worse......

Although no medications are currently available for treating marijuana abuse, recent discoveries about the working of the THC receptors have raised the possibility of eventually developing a medication that will block the intoxicating effects of THC. Such a medication might be used to prevent relapse to marijuana abuse by lessening or eliminating its appeal."[1]

And we hear they are considering legalizing this addictive drug. I believe it would be disaster for our nation. It is only the schemes of the devil that would cause it to even be considered, except for medicinal purposes. Given all the effects of marijuana on the brain and lungs, it would seem to me that common sense would keep it from being legalized. It seems that marijuana is the doorway for harder, more destructive drugs. Rob's addiction led him on to experiment with other drugs, cocaine being the most destructive.

It is too accessible now for even the youngest of children. Can you imagine the consequences of this drug being more freely available and not having any legal repercussions?

You might be interested in some information on cocaine and its effects taken from <u>Tips for Teens</u> online:

The Truth About Cocaine. "It is often referred to as Coke, Dust, Toot, Snow, Blow, Sneeze, Powder, Lines, and Rock (Crack)

Cocaine affects your brain. The word "cocaine" refers to the drug in both a powder (cocaine) and crystal (crack) form. It is made from the coca plant and causes a short-lived high that is immediately followed by opposite, intense feelings of depression, edginess, and a craving for more of the drug. Cocaine may be snorted as a powder, converted to a liquid form for injection with a needle, or processed into a crystal form to be smoked.

Cocaine affects your body. People who use cocaine often don't eat or sleep regularly. They can experience increased heart rate, muscle spasms, and convulsions. If they snort cocaine, they can also permanently damage their nasal tissue.

Cocaine affects your emotions. Using cocaine can make you feel paranoid, angry, hostile, and anxious, even when you're not high.

Cocaine is addictive. Cocaine interferes with the way your brain processes chemicals that create feelings of pleasure, so you need more and more of the drug just to feel normal. People who become addicted to cocaine start to lose interest in other areas of their lives, such as school, friends, and sports.

Cocaine can kill you. Cocaine use can cause heart attacks, seizures, strokes, and respiratory failure. People who share needles can also contract hepatitis, HIV/AIDs, or other diseases.

Cocaine is expensive. Regular users can spend hundreds and even thousands of dollars on cocaine each week. It impairs your judgment, which may lead to unwise decisions around sexual activity. This can increase your risk for HIV/AIDS, other diseases, rape, and unplanned pregnancy.

- How can you tell if a friend or loved one is using?
- Red, bloodshot eyes
- A runny nose or frequent sniffing
- A change in groups of friends
- Acting withdrawn, depressed, tired, or careless about personal appearance
- Losing interest in school, family, or activities he or she used to enjoy
- Frequently needing money

What can you do to help someone who is using cocaine? Be a real friend. Save a life. Encourage your friend to stop or seek professional help."[2]

The trouble is that in so many cases they will not heed the advice or will promise to go for help and then not follow through. If the addiction has a real hold on them, it is so hard to get a grip and reach out for help. You can see this on the TV program, "Intervention", as families attempt to convince their loved ones that they need the help offered. The person has to come to the point they want release from this stronghold for themselves. Many addicts have told me that even their children weren't enough to stop the craving they had. One man told me he literally lifted his little girl up and away from the refrigerator door to be able to get his beer out.

I once had a conversation with a prison guard and I shared that our son had been on cocaine. Her statement was, "No one gets off that drug." The Lord reminded me of our key verse, **"Nothing is impossible with God."** I have since heard the testimonies of many who have been able to walk away from their addictive behavior, including cocaine and heroin, as the Lord brought healing to them.

I watched a documentary on TV one night that showed the addictive brain. After watching that segment, the Lord helped me to understand that the addict does not think the way we do and it has helped me to understand them in a way that gives me the desire to help them come just as they are to the cross in order to find freedom from captivity. God is the only One Who can fill the void in their hearts, replacing it with His love and acceptance.

> *Prayer: Lord, we lift up anyone addicted to the substances we have listed above. We know these people have such a stronghold of the enemy in their lives that they think they can never be free, but we know You are the one who came to set the captives free. We believe that nothing is impossible with You, Amen*

CHAPTER FIFTEEN

Tragedy Strikes Once Again

**"It is good for me that I have been afflicted, that I might learn Your statutes."
Psalm 119:71, (AMP).**

As another chapter begins, we are sitting in the hospital as my husband, Jimmy, prepares to have his gallbladder surgery. He was admitted to the hospital the night before his surgery to receive antibiotics in preparation for the surgery because of infection. We were visiting with friends and a pastor friend who stopped by, but we were in no distress about the procedure.

As the friends departed that night I prepared to leave for home. I wanted to get a good night's rest because the following day would be a long day of waiting and care giving. I got home, did some chores, read as I often do to unwind and to hear a Word from the Lord before retiring for the night.

I was rudely awakened at 6:00 a. m. with the phone ringing. Jimmy's Dad, "Coot", answered on the other end of the line stating that he had run over Lucille, his wife, and "she was hurt bad". I immediately sat straight up in bed with disbelief. Thoughts ran through my mind that it couldn't be too bad. Maybe he had just hit her leg or her arm, but surely it was a very small accident that could be easily corrected. This was proof once again that one phone call can literally change your life!

Coot put their neighbor on the line, and she told me that Lucille was badly hurt and she was asking where they should take her. They lived in a rural area without much in the way of medical facilities. She asked if she should be transported to the local hospital or to Pinehurst which was about an hour from their home. I asked if they could come to Winston-Salem with her, so that I could take care of both she and Jimmy. She said the ambulance drivers said she was too bad to go that far, so it was decided that she would be taken to Pinehurst.

Our daughter, Melissa, was visiting my parents in Fayetteville, North Carolina. I called my Dad and shared the unbelievable news. He said they would meet us at the hospital in Pinehurst. I knew they would be able to get there before we could so I was grateful for that blessing.

After a multitude of phone calls to family members, I called my husband's doctor and told him the situation because I knew Jimmy would want to go and asked if we could do that. He wanted Jimmy to have one specific test before he left and told me he would make the arrangements with the nurses to get his personal care accomplished while I hastened to pick him up for our unexpected trip.

When we got to the hospital I told Jimmy the tragic news, and of course he was ready to leave the hospital immediately. The nurses came to discontinue his IV. We got him changed into his clothes and into the car in no time. It seemed like a very long trip with all that was at stake for us. It probably took us a good hour and a half. In that sort of situation, minutes seem like hours.

As we reached the hospital, we found it hard to find where the family was waiting. Finally we were directed to the surgical waiting area where we discovered that Jimmy's Mother was in surgery. They had already come out to let them know that she had coded once.

She had a broken pelvis, a ruptured bladder, and other injuries. It did not sound promising that she would live through this accident. I will never forget the tension of the moment with family and friends waiting to hear word, expecting the worst possible news but hoping for the best. The tension in the air was so thick it was almost unbearable.

Jimmy's Dad, Coot, was in shock. He said, "I never killed anyone before." It was so sad watching him suffer the agony of what had happened. Jimmy was so desperate to hear news of his Mother's condition but afraid of what he would hear at the same time.

God allowed us time to get to the hospital, but it was probably less than fifteen minutes after we arrived that the surgeon came out to tell us that she was gone. She just had too many injuries, and she had two cardiac arrests on the operating table. They were unable to revive her.

Coot wanted to see her, so we all went together and saw that her face was very swollen. I wished at the time that we had not seen her, but he needed to see her, and I can understand that. It was so hard to believe that one moment they were on their way for a pleasurable day trip and the next we found ourselves in an emergency room hearing the worst news we could have imagined.

Melissa shared later that she was able to be with Grandma before they took her to surgery. She wasn't able to talk, but she blinked her eyes in recognition of her presence and squeezed her hand. I know it was most reassuring to her to know that Melissa was there. God knew that she would be needed, and I honestly believe He had her in place to get there quickly to have those last moments with her.

We had tried several times to share our faith with Jimmy's parents, and they would become offended and change the subject. They were good people and brought him up in church for years, but as Jimmy remembered, he never heard the plan of salvation in his little church and did not know you had to invite Jesus to come into your heart.

It was after we started dating and he went with me to our church that he heard the Gospel presented by my father during the service and walked the aisle to accept Christ as his Savior afterwards.

Of course this was on our minds in hopes that his Mother had made things right with the Father before she passed that day. It would feel better to know for sure, but we pray we will one day see her again running to meet us in our heavenly home.

We questioned at this time why everything in our life seemed to be so dramatic and tragic. Lord, we don't pretend to understand but we trust you.

In my quiet time I came to **Psalm 67:1-2a (NKJV), "God be merciful to us and bless us, and cause His face to shine upon us. That Your way may be known on earth."**

Psalm 61:1-4 (NKJV) states **"Hear my cry, O God; attend to my prayer. From the end of the earth I will cry to You, when my heart is overwhelmed; lead me to the rock that is higher than I. For You have been a shelter for me, a strong tower from the enemy. I will abide in Your tabernacle forever".**

Family and friends were in and out of the Kearns's home bringing food, flowers, fruit baskets, words of encouragement, and promises of prayers. Coot was still in shock and visited with each one as if nothing had happened. We had so many friends from our church and work to come from our hometown to the visitation at the funeral home. It was overwhelming the love that each one showed. Lord, you bless us with the presence of such wonderful friends. They are truly a demonstration of Your love for us. You aren't here on earth in a physical sense, but we can feel Your loving arms around us through the love expressed by our friends.

Jimmy had requested that our dear friend Cathy sing for his Mother's funeral. She did a wonderful job as she sang out of love for us. Bless her for what she did that day to encourage us with song. The words of the songs were certainly a comfort to us as she sang God's praises. What a reminder to praise God no matter our circumstances.

My Dad spoke in the service along with the pastor of the church. He did such a great job and of course shared the gospel. He brought some very encouraging words to the family and we will always remember my parent's support during such a trying time.

My dear friend, Joan, called with some scripture to encourage us on that day of the funeral. It was from **Psalm 145:14-21(NKJV):**

"The LORD upholds all who fall, and raises up all who are bowed down. The eyes of all look expectantly to You, and You give them their food in due season. You open Your hand and satisfy the desire of every living thing. The LORD is righteous in all His ways, gracious in all His works. The LORD is near to all who call upon Him, To all who call upon Him in truth. He will fulfill the desire of those who fear Him; He also will hear their cry and save them. The LORD preserves all who love Him, but all the wicked He will destroy. My mouth shall speak the praise of the LORD, and all flesh shall bless His holy name forever and ever."

After the funeral, everyone had left and it was quiet in the household. I had a chance to go to my Bible and came to this passage**: "My eyes are ever toward the LORD, for He shall pluck my feet out of the net. Turn Yourself to me, and have mercy on me, for I am desolate and afflicted. The troubles of my heart have enlarged; bring me out of my distresses! Look on my affliction and my pain, and forgive all my sins. Consider my enemies, for they are many; and they hate me with cruel hatred. Keep my soul, and deliver me; let me not be ashamed, for I put my trust in You. Let integrity and uprightness preserve me, for I wait for You. Redeem Israel, O God, out of all their troubles!" Psalm 25:15-22 (NKJV).**

How many times have the Psalms described the utter pain and agony in my heart? I can relate so much to some of the passages that David wrote in his bouts with the enemy. He didn't always understand the reason for his situations either, but he continued to trust His Lord and Master in all things. I will choose to do the same.

Once again Rob could not be with his family in this very trying time. When we returned home, I went to the jail to tell him of the loss of his Grandma. All he could do was pound on the windows that separated us, and cry. We could not console each other with even the touch of a hand. What a horrible way to grieve the loss of a loved one!

Since the death of Jimmy's Mother, his Dad has been going downhill. He has bouts of depression and his physical well-being has not been good for a very long time. We brought him home with us for a couple of weeks and he seemed to eat better and perked up some but misses home and his friends.

We have made many trips to his hometown, Troy over the past few months with emergency room visits with problems with his congestive heart failure, bleeding from an undetermined origin, and one night we could not get his nose to stop bleeding because he was taking a blood thinner. We had to take him to the ED to get help with the continued bleeding.

We took Coot to see Robbie when he had a better day. Jimmy told Robbie that this would probably be the last time he ever saw his grandfather because we could see the inevitable. This was a very hard, trying time for Jimmy as he was still grieving the death of his Mother. Once again Robbie will not be able to be with the family during this hard period we are facing.

We were able to find a brand new assisted living facility close to Coot's home. He agreed he needed more care and he wanted to remain in his hometown area so his friends could come visit him. As nice as the facility was, we found it hard to leave him there.

It hadn't been but a few days when we received a call at 5:30 in the morning reporting that Coot had fallen between his bed and nightstand and had a laceration on his face and head. He had laid there for some time before he was found. The facility had taken him to the emergency department. He had had his head all bandaged up when we got there to see him. He looked like he had been in a major cat fight and ended up the worse for it.

His condition continued to worsen and once again we found ourselves in the hospital with a diagnosis of congestive heart failure, pulmonary disease, and renal failure. Coot had already had three heart attacks and heart by-pass surgery. We knew his heart was weak.

In my quiet time with the Lord this morning he took me to **I Kings 2:1a (KJV), "Now the days of David drew near that he should die."** I believe I heard that one loud and clear. We stayed all night in the hospital waiting area with trips in to see him in ICU when we allowed to. No matter how prepared you think you are for the loss of a loved one, it is never easy even if we know the body is deteriorating.

The next day the Doctor reported that there had not been much change. He does seem a little more alert and talkative. He wants to get out of bed and walk, but he is just too weak. I know with the fight he has to live he wants to just get up and walk down the hall in his own strength hoping to beat the clock that is ticking away his life.

The nurses came in to turn his oxygen down to see if he could tolerate it, but he couldn't. They had to increase the liters within a short period of time. It is so hard to watch him struggling for each breath.

The doctor decided to release Coot from ICU today. Ironic that it is his birthday. He always loved his birthdays and receiving cards and gifts. He was always like a little boy as he tore into his gifts or looked for a piece of money to fall from his cards.

We were able to go home and do some errands and get some rest for a day or two. Then we went back to Albemarle to see Coot at the hospital. The cardiologist reports that they are having trouble keeping the fluid off his lungs and his kidneys are functioning poorly. He is not eating or drinking much at all. Several friends and family came in and out during the course of the day to offer their support.

As I sat with Coot he did not talk much at all. I read Psalm 23 to him quietly. I tried to encourage him that Jesus was walking with him through the valley. I reminded him of the promises of a heavenly body, free from pain and suffering. I asked him again if he was sure he had made things right with God, he nodded yes.

A couple of nights later Jimmy went down to see his Dad by himself and he said his Dad was like his old self, entertaining everyone present. Coot said twice that, "People get better before they die". That does seem to ring true in so many instances. I have often seen that happen as a nurse.

As we were celebrating Melissa's birthday we received a call that Coot's doctor had been in and said he had developed pneumonia and probably would not make it over the week-end. We all got together and breathed a word of prayer for him and we specifically asked that he not pass on Melissa's birthday. I didn't want her to remember her birthday with that loss each year to come. God did honor that prayer for which we are so grateful.

Jimmy and I gathered our things, said our good-byes and left for the hospital. By this time Coot is in a private room and we spent the night with him. He was getting weaker and weaker. I called Melissa the next morning and told her that if she wanted to speak to him she better come on because it would not be long. She and Bryan arrived in the next couple of hours.

We all sat in the room sharing about old times as a family when I looked over and saw that Coot's respirations were very shallow and longer in between. As I get up to go get the nurse, he slips out of this life of struggle. He has fought a good fight.

I cannot imagine the pain Jimmy is experiencing due to the loss of both parents in such a short time. It is a loss no one can comprehend unless they have experienced it. Being an only child, it means his only family is us now. It is so sad to think about. It makes our little family even more precious to us. I thank God for our wonderful children and grandchildren. What would life be without them? I don't want to imagine!

We have been blessed to get our granddaughters as much as we would like and take them to see their Daddy. We want them to bond so we make every effort to get them there to visit with him. We have to time everything just right with feeding and diaper changes since they won't let you take in diapers or milk in the bottle. It is hard to keep them entertained for the two hours there because they have to stay at your table.

We take the girls to church when we have them and they love to go to Sunday School. I hope to expose them to the Word and that they will know the love of their Heavenly Father as much as possible. Maybe one day their earthly father will be a part of their lives. I love them with all my heart and know they are a gift from God to us in filling the void we experienced as our son went off to prison.

I thank their mother, Tina, for allowing us the privilege of having the girls so much. We have tried to honor my promise to help with them over the years. Our family cannot imagine life without Carolyn and Shelbi. They liven up the house and bring much joy and love to us.

Right after the other losses, Rob called us one evening with the news that he has been having some health issues and he had gone to the prison Dr. who told him he didn't like what he saw. He apparently has a mass in his testicle and he is going to send him for an MRI. He thinks there is a chance that it may be testicular cancer. None of us wants to hear those words in regards to a loved one especially our child, but God gave me peace about it.

In my quiet time the next morning I came to **Genesis 22:2a (KJV)," And He said, Take now thy son, thine only son, Isaac whom thou lovest"**, ----not in a year, not a month or week, but now. I will chose to lay our son on His altar and allow Him to do the work He needs to do. **"In the day when I cried thou answeredst me and strengthened me with strength in my soul." Psalm 138:3 (KJV).**

I thank you Lord for giving me strength to turn over our son to You once again.

It has taken a long time to get the test done but I know it comes in God's timing. The Dr. has encouraged Rob to go ahead and have the surgery to remove the testicle because even if it is not cancer it could cause him problems down the road so the surgery is arranged. Of course, since he is a prisoner his family cannot know the exact date or time of the surgery and that will be hard for us not to be there with him. It is just another example of the new normal of a prisoner's family.

The doctor called to say things went very well with the procedure and Rob will return to his old camp soon. Each time I hope and pray that this will be the turning point in his walk back to the Father so we wait to see. Whatever happens I know God is working!

The next morning I was looking for the name of the Father to give to a friend as comfort in a trying time and the Lord took me to the name Jehovah-Shammah, the Lord is there. I knew God was reminding me that even though we could not be with him, He was. What a comfort for me.

> *Prayer: Lord, so many times we don't understand Your plan, but we pray we will always trust Your hand as You allow afflictions for Your purposes. You say in Your Word, "It is good for me that I have been afflicted; that I might learn your statutes." Psalm: 119:71. Continue to teach us Your statutes, and may we learn the lessons You have for us in our times of suffering, Amen.*

CHAPTER SIXTEEN

A Divine Appointment in the Middle East

"Then I heard the voice of the LORD saying, 'Whom shall I send, and who will go for Us!' Then I said, "Here am I. Send me! And He said, "Go and tell the people" Isaiah 6:8-9 (NAS).

The war is raging in Iraq, and we see almost play by play what is taking place through the live news reports on television. I see the blank, hurting faces of the people of that nation and can only imagine the agony they are enduring under the rule of a wicked and evil government. Their leader's goal is to keep the people oppressed while government officials live in palaces and eat of the delicacies of the land. No matter your political stand on the war, I believe it is a spiritual war just like the tearing down of the Berlin Wall. God is penetrating the area with the Truth and is bringing freedom to many held captive to the torture of evil men.

So, when the call was put forth in our church for those willing to go to Iraq on mission, I was drawn to the informational meeting. My family was shocked and was not so sure that I should go into a war zone.

Days later Jimmy and I left for a conference at the Cove in Asheville, NC. While waiting for the seminar to begin, I opened my Bible and read, **"Then I heard the voice of the LORD saying, "Whom shall I send, and who will go for Us? Then I said, 'Here am I. Send me!' And He said go and tell the** people." **Isaiah 6:8-9 (NAS)**. I knew in my Spirit that He was calling me. Even the songs that were sung spoke to me-----to follow Him.

One song we sang at the Cove is now a prayer of commitment from me to the Lord:

> **"Take my heart and form it**
> **Take my mind, transform it**
> **Take my will, conform it**
> **To Yours, to Yours, O, Lord."**

All these scriptures I received as promises of the Father for the trip:

I Corinthians 15:58 (NKJV), "Therefore, my beloved brethren, be steadfast, immovable, always abounding in the work of the Lord, knowing that your labor is not in vain in the Lord."

Isaiah 45:2-3 (NKJV) states, **"I will go before you and make the crooked places straight; I will break in pieces the gates of bronze, and cut the bars of iron. I will give you the treasures of darkness and hidden riches of secret places, That you may know that I, the LORD, Who call you by your name, Am the God of Israel."**

I continue to hear reports of soldiers being killed, and of course it makes me a little nervous. One night I received an email from a friend which read: "If God brings me to it, He will bring me through it! May today there be peace within you. May you trust God that you are exactly where you are meant to be."

As in times before when I have gone on mission with God, He has provided through gifts from others. This time my daughter and her husband sent me a generous gift with promises of prayers. Support continued from many others also.

My family is very concerned, but at the same time they know by now that when God calls we must obey no matter the circumstances or dangers. There are more and more reports of car bombings, soldiers being killed, and some harm even to the contractors over there trying to help rebuild and repair.

Food boxes that are donated and packed by our church members are being sent over for us to distribute while we are there. The people have such physical needs, and we must meet some of those before we begin to share with them about the love of Christ. They have to see his love demonstrated through us first.

We are days away from leaving for our trip, and the news reports on the announcement of a bombing in Iraq of the U. N. building, the Red

Cross and a bombing in Israel by a suicide bomber. Security is tight, and I am wondering if we will even be able to go to Iraq. The Lord is in control I assure myself.

My friend, Phyliss, called with the following scripture from **Exodus 3:7-10 (NAS): "Then the Lord told him, "You can be sure I have seen the affliction of My people in *[Iraq]*, and have given heed to their cry because their taskmasters, for I am aware of their sufferings. So I have come down to deliver them from the power of *[Iraq]* and to bring them up from that land to a good and spacious land, to a land flowing with milk and honey,-...... The cries of the people of *[Iraq]* have reached Me, and I have seen how the [government] have oppressed them with heavy tasks. Therefore, come now, and I will send you to Pharoah, so that you, may bring My people, the sons of *[Iraq's]* out of *[Iraq]*." Emphasis *(mine)*** Moses made excuses because he felt inadequate for the job God asked him to do, but God wasn't asking Moses to work alone. He offered Moses other resources to help. God often calls us to do tasks that seem too difficult, but He doesn't ask us to do them alone.

Less than a week before our mission, we had an emergency meeting regarding our trip. We were informed that we will not be able to go into Iraq. The security level was such that we were prohibited from traveling to Iraq at this time. Everyone was disappointed and couldn't understand why the door had been closed to us. We had done so much planning and preparation to go into the country where we felt called.

We were asked if we still wanted to go to another area and take food boxes to the people there. We didn't know what purpose the Father had in all this, but we trusted Him. We all agreed; we still wanted to go. We had a time of prayer together and cried our hearts out because we had so wanted to minister to the Iraqi people.

As we rolled out onto the tarmac I looked out my window, and there stood two doves. God was with us. We got out on the runway and were told we would have to wait for clearance to take off because of the weather.

We went back to the area where the workers had loaded the plane, and they opened the baggage compartment and began taking luggage off the plane and loaded it onto the baggage cart. I began to pray, as I know the others did, that we would be able to get off the ground to connect with our flight in New York on time. Time was slipping away, and it was beginning to look like we would not arrive at our destination on time.

In the next five minutes I observed that the men were placing the bags back on the plane, and it looked like we might indeed depart. I read

Romans 8:34 where Christ is making intercession for us. **Romans 8:31b (KJV)** provided reassurance, too. **"If God be for us, who can be against us?"** How reassuring is that!

We taxied out on to the runway over an hour later than anticipated. We would have to go through customs on arrival for an international flight which might take a while, so we continued to pray that we would make our connection in time to proceed to our destination.

God provided a place to stay for us, which was right beside the community school. We went up on the roof to have an overview of the surrounding area. I was glad we had this getaway so that I could be alone with the Lord for some quiet time. It reminded me of the stories in the Bible when the people went up on their roofs.

I knew that this was not where we planned or hoped to be, but God knew it all along. We discovered that there are many Iraqee refugees in this city, and we were going to have our food boxes arrive with a great deal of supplies for us to distribute at some point. It was also decided that we would purchase lots of staple goods here in this country to give out to the folks as God directed.

We were going to Petra and were driven by a couple who lived in the area. They worked to provide opportunities for us to take the food boxes in the place God had sent us. The rock was carved out into the most amazing lost city. Some of the carved monuments that we saw had inscriptions that told what they were used for. Most were tombs, some were dwellings, some were used as temples and places of worship, and others as rooms to prepare the dead for burial.

We were approached by many Bedouin children with wares for sale. They were sometimes very small children, and we were told that their parents were probably hiding out and watching as the children attempted to sell and bring them the profits. Some of the Bedouin people lived and found quick shelter in the caves of the rocks. We were told some of the women enter the rocks to have their children.

In **II Kings 14:7 (NIV)** it refers to Petra, **"He was the one who defeated ten thousand Edomites in the Valley of Salt and captured Sela in battle, calling it Joktheel, the name it has to this day."** Another name for Petra is Sela-rock, a city carved out of sheer mountain walls located about 50 miles south of the Dead Sea.

As we were coming back down from Petra, we stopped for a picnic outside of Mt. Nebo. Afterwards we walked up to the top of the mountain where there is a memorial to Moses. On one side of the building, we looked out and stood possibly on the spot where Moses looked into the Promised Land, where God told him he would not be able to go into the land. It made me grieve as the writing took me back to that day and experience. I know Moses' heart must have broken to know he could not enter with his people. What an awesome experience to stand in a place where the great prophet stood! I have read and been told the story of Moses all my life. I never dreamed I would have such an awesome experience.

Melinda, one of my prayer partners, and I were able to sit on the wall overlooking Israel and the surrounding land as we prayed over our trip and the people in the beloved city of God. Afterwards we went to dinner in an outdoor setting looking over Israel, Syria, and Turkey, and the Sea of Galilee. Little did I know that I would be called back to a country close by the next year. Following God is the most exciting journey I know of.

I mentioned that we were staying at the home which joined to the property of the area school. We were able to go and help them with projects and anything they needed us to do, whether that was teaching a class, reading to the children during their library time, making up bulletins boards, or laminating learning tools for their future use. When given the assignment of making up bulletin boards, I was way out of my comfort zone, but God brought ideas and materials to get it accomplished. It was fun watching the children come by and make comments about it later.

I got up during the middle of the night with an upset stomach, so I must have eaten something which has given me dysentery. I was so upset because the ladies in our group were planning to go to the Iraqi women's clinic that day, and I was afraid I was not going to be able to go. I began to feel a little better before the departure time, so I got up and took a shower, dressed, and lay back down to rest and made sure I was strong enough to go. When we arrived, the whole yard was filled to overflow with Iraqi ladies and their children. We had brought diapers, formula, baby wipes, and some food for each one. I walked into the clinic and had to go into the office and sit down because I felt waves of nausea envelop me. It was very hot outside, and the curvy ride up the mountain had unsettled me. I was so embarrassed that I had to heave into the office trash can, but I absolutely could not help it. The office personnel assisted me along with some of my own fellow travelers.

I will never forget one lady who came and sat down beside me and literally wiped my brow and mouth and put her hand of compassion on me. She left at one point and I believed I would not see her again but about 30 minutes later she came back in the door holding a package and opened it to give me. It was a pack of wipes and she wanted me to have the whole pack.

I didn't know how far she traveled from home or how much it had cost her. Here we were trying to minister to them and she ministered to me in a way that overwhelmed me. As I left, she told me she loved me and asked me to please come back someday.

I just couldn't believe that I was sick, and I cried out to the Father to bring relief because I wanted to be about His business. There was much to do, and I didn't want to be laid up in the bed! Our team took turns each day going out in groups to visit the homes, take food, and hopefully have an opportunity to tell them of God's love.

I was in the last group to go out because I had been sick, but I had been looking forward to visiting the people in their home. As my van left to make visits, we stopped at a nearby store and bought supplies like cooking oil, rice, and flour to take to the homes.

We stopped at a home, and the interpreter with us went down the steps into a home where an aunt and her niece were housed to see if it would be okay to visit. The rest of the families were all at work. Our leader asked permission for us to come bring them some food. He came back to the van and told us we could go in but that only the two ladies were home. We all agreed that we should go in.

When we entered, the ladies were preparing us an orange drink. As with other international trips I have taken, we have always been told not to drink from their cups because of the possibility of becoming ill, but it was just disrespectful not to partake when they so graciously offered it to you.

As we began to talk through the interpreter, I noticed that the lady seemed very troubled over something she was sharing with him. He began to explain to us that this mother had come to Jordan to help her son who was in prison with murder charges. She declared that he was not guilty and was attempting to receive help to get him out or at least be heard.

I knew in my spirit as soon as she started speaking that God had called me to Iraq but stopped us in this place, if for no other reason than to minister to this mother. This was my destiny for this trip. She was heartbroken, and tears began to roll down her cheeks. I was overwhelmed with her pain and the emotion of the moment. I began to tell her that I also had a son in prison and I knew her anguish and sense of helplessness. I was able to share how God had brought me through some very difficult days and had sent me encouragement to never give up.

I was privileged to pray with her as we reached for each other's hand in a sense of comradeship of spirit and empathy of heart. It was a moment I will never forget. It blew my mind that even way down in the basement of a tiny home so far from mine; God had so much love and concern for a hurting mother that He sent me to encourage her. He had orchestrated the whole thing. If I had not been sick days before, I might have gone out for my turn and missed my calling. Praise Him for His marvelous love and wisdom. Help me, Lord, to never question what You allow in my life.

Another day we were able to go out as a group and prayer walk the streets downtown. In my quiet time before going God gave me, **"So I will strengthen them in the LORD, and they shall walk up and down in His name",** **says the Lord."** This is found in **Zechariah 10:12 (NKJV).**

We had dinner in two or three of our new found friends' homes. They showed us so much hospitality. It was amazing. We met one national who had been called to go into Baghdad to minister to the people and was going to be leaving in a couple of days with his family.

For the first time people would be baptized publicly in Baghdad. Wow! People are being set free, not only from the oppression of evil rulers, but also from the oppression of Satan. Whoever calls upon the name of Christ will be free indeed!

We went into the home of another family, and the teenage girl had cystic fibrosis. She was so pale and so frail. She had several episodes of coughing while we visited. She got up and went to her little corner of the room and brought each of us ladies a picture she had drawn. One of them had a bird on it, and I asked her if it was a dove and she said, "Yes." I had a dove pin on my blouse, and I felt impressed to give it to her. I pinned it on her, and she just beamed. I told her when she wore it to remember that we were praying for her. We talked and laughed together, and the mother of the girl spoke to the interpreter and told him it was the happiest day of her life that we had come. Oh, do we know how fortunate we are to have family with whom we can laugh and have all the provisions we need. Sometimes I think we are too busy and too into the TV to enjoy the company of each other. One of the ladies with us had an inhaler, and she was able to leave it with the young lady. God just kept providing everywhere we went. Jehovah Rapha, touch this young lady.

As our time came to an end, it was with mixed emotions that we said our good-byes and packed up to return home. I turned to **Ecclesiastes 3:12-13 (NAS), "I know that there is nothing better for them than to rejoice and to do good in one's lifetime moreover, that every man who eats and drinks sees**

good in all his labor—it is the gift of God." The accompanying commentary reads: "In accepting everything as a gift of his Creator, even in a cursed world, man is enabled to see 'good' in all his work."

> *Prayer: Lord, I thank you that you have such love and compassion for each of us that You arrange to bring someone across the waters to minister to the hurting heart of a mother who was suffering such agony over her son. You minister Your healing touch through those willing to go when You call. Often plans are changed to accomplish Your purposes. Thank you for allowing me to be a part of what you are doing. You continue to amaze me, Lord, Amen.*

CHAPTER SEVENTEEN

Sing a New Song

"Sing to Him a new song; play skillfully with a shout of joy" Psalm 33:3, (NAS).

For the past year or so, God has been telling me to sing a new song. I have been responding, "Lord, you know I can't sing. Every time I open my mouth to sing, those within ear shot, especially my family, quickly say, 'Stop'. Sometimes even my grandchildren at the age of three respond the same way." (Of course their Paw Paw didn't have anything to do with that I am sure!)

I received a note from my spiritual mentor, Joan, which reads as follows:

Psalm 40:3 (NAS), "And He put a new song in my mouth, a song of praise to our God; Many shall see and fear, and will trust in the LORD." She continues, "If the Holy Spirit is coaxing a new song from you, then open your mouth. In denying this, we deny the work of the Holy Spirit in the lives of others. Ears that wait will not hear what perhaps will set them free. Our new song is never intended for us alone."

Don't allow responsibilities to suffocate our dreams. We can mask His purpose; even suffocate it by our hectic pace. Winston Churchill said,

"Courage is the capacity to go from failure to failure without losing your enthusiasm."

Psalm 144:9 (NKJV) reads, **"I will sing a new song to You, O God; on a harp of ten strings I will sing praises to You."** This is a song of deliverance by David on the day God delivered him from his enemies and from the hand of Saul.

From this point on, David lives above his troubles. He takes his stand on the highlands of faith. His determination to sing a new song is picked up by the Holy Spirit and carried through by him to the end of the Psalm.

There are other scriptures which focus on a new song:

Psalm 149:1 (NIV), "Praise the Lord! Sing to the Lord a new song, and His praise in the assembly of saints."

Isaiah 42:10a (AMP), "Sing to the Lord a new song, and His praise from the end of the earth!"

In Exodus 15, Moses and the children of Israel sang a song to the Lord because He had delivered them from the Egyptians. As you see, the singing took place after some kind of deliverance and was a song of praise to the Lord who brought those out of some bondage or wilderness experience.

God does not bring us through adversity or a wilderness experience without giving us a song to sing for His glory. Look at Moses who spent 40 years on the backside of the desert and came out singing praises to the Lord.

Look at David who was anointed King of the Jews, killed the enemy Goliath, yet spent the next few years shepherding the sheep, and then running from Saul for his very life. What would it be like without the songs of praise David wrote during and after his deliverance from his enemies? Maybe you have found yourself in a desert or wilderness experience for what has been literally 40 years or more. What song of praise is He calling you to sing because of what He has brought you through?

Our time of waiting may be a time of breaking, teaching, molding, breaking again, and then being remolded until the Potter crafts us into a usable vessel. Oh yes, the breaking must occur in order for Him to use us and grow us, just like the seed placed in the ground must break open to bring new life forth. Praise God, He doesn't just sweep those broken pieces of vessel into the trash but He is able to help us pick up the pieces and make us useful again even when we have come crashing down.

As I write this, I am sitting on my screened-in porch, and it could not be a more beautiful day to write. The sun is shining beautifully, and there is a gently blowing breeze. The beauty of the dogwoods, azaleas, and bright purple irises are breathtaking. It is a time of new beginnings. I am reminded of our Elohim who created the world and all the beauty we are privileged to enjoy. His hand is seen in each intricate detail of nature. The birds can be heard in song; even the rustle of the trees blowing in the wind sounds like a song.

God reminds me of the passage which says that if we do not sing out praises to Him, the very stones will. Let's never neglect to give Him the praise which is due Him.

In **Song of Solomon 2:10-13 (NKJV), "My beloved spoke, and said to me: Rise up, my love, my fair one, and come away. For lo, the winter is past, the rain is over and gone. The flowers appear on the earth; the time of singing has come, and the voice of the turtledove is heard in our land. The fig tree puts forth her green fig, and the vines with the tender grapes give a good smell. Rise up, my love, my fair one, and come away!"** This passage is a call to come forth out of our box so to speak and to rise above our own personal circumstances and enjoy the fellowship of our Lord no matter the trial or testing we may be in. He wants us to abide in Him and trust Him to bring us through.

You may be coming out of the winter, spiritually speaking, in your life. What do you think of when you think of winter? Those days are gloomy, dark, and cold, and there is no growth. There are decreased opportunities to work outside. So now He bids his beloved to come out because winter has passed.

Springtime is a time of resurrection life. That is what we see in spring as the plants pop up out of the ground with new growth and beauty, and the trees bloom and we are captured by the fragrance of them all. We are encouraged by what we see and what we experience in our soul when we are renewed.

Does it mean that storms won't sometimes blow in and cause destruction and leave their mark? No, but we learn that despite the storm God allows us to come through, He is Sovereign and in absolute control of them. He walks with us in the storm, sometimes even carrying us in His loving arms or over His shoulder as He did the lost lamb. That is the picture I like to imagine. I see myself cradled in His arms, leaning on His bosom just as the Word pictures John the beloved leaning on Him at the Last Supper.

So, just as the birds sing their song and the wind sings as it calmly blows, we are to sing sweet praises to the Lord for His faithfulness in our seasons of winter. Many times though, what He hears instead are our groans and complaints. We come out of our trials questioning God instead of praising Him for all He has done in our situation and in us. It is tempting to harbor bitterness and anger at God instead of seeing Him working in us to break us and mold us into His vessel for His purposes.

Sometimes I do think that I have needed a lot of breaking in my life. How about you? We can have hope spiritually that the winter will pass and that spring is coming. Then as we sing His praises, we spread forth a sweet smelling fragrance, pleasing unto Him. If we groan, moan, and complain, we put forth a fragrance that is foul and overpowering.

Ever met anyone who sends out a foul smell of bitterness, self-pity, and unforgiveness, always blaming others? Just examine yourself, and make sure the foul smell you detect is not coming from yourself.

I want to be found like a sweet smelling savor sending out the fragrance of Jesus and most importantly letting my life send forth a sweet fragrance to my Lord, therefore bringing Him glory.

I see the writing of this book as a new song to the faithfulness of my Father. I have much to praise Him for. He has been my counselor, my provider, my sustainer, my Savior, my Abba Father, and my hope, and I praise Him for helping me to see I have songs to sing even through the pain and sorrows of life.

I will close this chapter with the song of Miriam found in **Exodus 15:20 (AMP):**

"Then Miriam the prophetess, the sister of Aaron, took the timbrel in her hand; and all the women went out after her with timbrels and dancing. And Miriam responded to them:

> **Sing to the Lord,**
> **For He has triumphed gloriously**
> **And is highly exalted;**
> **The horse and its rider**
> **He was thrown into the sea!"**

Start singing your own new song unto the Lord. He deserves all our praise and worship. He is the King of kings, the Lord of lords, the great I Am, and most of all our Abba Father.

Prayer: Lord, You have taught me to sing new songs to You, my Deliverer and Friend, over the years in spite of my circumstances. *What joy to know that You hear my praises and actually enjoy them as I sing out of the overflow from my heart with thanksgiving for how You have brought me through many battles, Amen.*

CHAPTER EIGHTEEN

Another Call to Go

"The Lord your God carried you, as a man carries his son, in all the way that you went until you came to this place" Deuteronomy 1:31b, (NKJV).

Melissa and Bryan announced to us that we were going to be the proud grandparents of a new baby due to arrive in February. As she told us, I almost choked on the wonton soup I was enjoying. After all, we had been waiting for this announcement for several years and had decided it might not happen. What an exciting time this was in the life of our family. So much shopping and planning to do! **Psalm 127:3b (NKJV), "The fruit of the womb is His reward."**

Around this same time, I felt led to go to another country in answer to the Lord's call. I was walking through the lobby of church one Sunday after the service, and a friend asked me if I was going to travel in December with the group. I explained that I didn't know about it. The next Sunday as I met someone in the hallway, they also asked me if I was going on the trip. As I left that day I said, "Okay Lord, if You are calling me to go, I will know it is You if one more person approaches me about it."

As I came out of the service the next Sunday after rounding up our granddaughters from Sunday school, the leader of the trip came out and asked, "Sandra, are you going on the trip with us?" My answer was, "I guess I am!"

The way God calls each time so differently is exciting to me. We must listen for His call to hear His voice in any situation because it may come differently.

Due to the sensitivity of the trip, it was not talked about much, but we had lots of meetings to plan and prepare. We all had to sign up for two different areas in which we wanted to serve while we were there on the field. Most were going to minister to the children much like Vacation Bible School.

I presented five things to my prayer partners to pray about:

1. Physical health and strength in the Lord.
2. Discernment and sensitivity to needs of the missionaries.
3. Conviction of any wrong motives or attitudes I might have.
4. Prayer to guard my thoughts and not sidetrack me with issues at home.
5. Protection of my family during my absence.

You see, I was leaving with the knowledge that our son, Robbie, could be arrested at any time. In years gone by I would not even have considered leaving town much less the country with all that was going on with him. I believed that God was in control of the situation, and I must be obedient to His call for my life and let Him do the work needed here at home.

Jimmy and I had discussed the fact that I would not ask when I called home, and he would not reveal any information regarding Robbie. I always found that it would totally distract me from what I had to do, so it was best to just leave it in the Father's hands. There was nothing I could do anyway, and once again I knew I was not in control; God was.

In my devotions days before we departed I was studying **Isaiah 41:10 (AMP)** which reads, **"Fear not; [there is nothing to fear] for I am with you; do not look around you in terror and be dismayed, for I am your God. I will strengthen and harden you to [difficulties]; yes, I will help you; yes, I will hold you up and retain you with My victorious right hand of rightness and justice."**

As I prepared to leave, my friends were encouraging me and promising to pray. My friend, Sandy, gave me a passage of scripture in **Isaiah 58: 10-11 (AMP)**, **"And if you pour out that with which you sustain your own life for the hungry, and satisfy the need of the afflicted, then shall your light rise in darkness and your obscurity and gloom be as the noonday. And the Lord** shall guide you continually, and satisfy you in drought and in dry places, and make strong your bones. And you shall be like a watered garden and like a spring of water, whose waters never fail."

I experienced much spiritual warfare in preparation for this trip, and on departure day I suffered with a terrible toothache. I have never had problems with my teeth. I decided I needed to have it checked that morning before I had to be at the church for the trip to the airport. Fortunately I did get an appointment and found I had a cracked tooth.

My dentist filled it, and I prayed the filling would last until my return to the United States. Thank you, Jesus, for arranging all the details to be worked out in time to make my way to the church.

On the plane I read **Psalm 91:2 (AMP), "I will say of the LORD, 'He is my refuge and my fortress, my God, on Him I lean and rely, and in Him I (confidently) trust!'"**

The Lord reminds me that He puts limits on my suffering. We can be confident that suffering will not last forever. **Psalm 30:4 (NIV) says, "Sing to the Lord, you saints of His; praise His holy name. For His anger lasts only a moment, but His favor lasts a lifetime; weeping may remain for a night, but rejoicing comes in the morning."** My Father knows that I leave with a heavy heart. Thank you, Jesus, that times of suffering are for my benefit and Your glory. What a comfort to know such times are privileges ordained by You to take me one step farther with You. I yield, knowing You will see me through.

The flight went smoothly, and we arrived at our destination safely. The motel was very nice. I was escorted to my room which I would call home for the next two weeks. I am roomed by myself and looked forward to the times I would have alone with my Lord. I went out on the balcony and looked to my left to see the beautiful blue Mediterranean Sea. It was an unbelievable sight for sore eyes. I couldn't wait to get out on that beach to walk and take in the magnificent glory of it all. I asked the Lord to let me find a few white stones to take back to my friends for a very special purpose.

You see, I was taken to a passage of scripture before leaving home that gave me the idea of writing **Revelation 2:17 (NAS)** on a white stone, **"He, who has an ear, let him hear what the Spirit says to the churches. To him who overcomes I will give some of the hidden manna to eat. And I will give him a white stone, and on the stone a new name written which no one knows except him who receives it."**

As my friend, Nora, and I walked out on the beach I was overwhelmed as I looked out and saw a million white stones and every other color imaginable. This beach did not have sand but very small pebbles and then larger stones of every color. I wanted the stone to be a reminder to my friends who are also going through struggles, that as we finish our race, we will be given a new name. It would be an encouragement to persevere in the race to the finish line and never give up on His promises. This would be my gift to them upon my return home.

When an athlete won in the games, he was often given, as part of his prize, a white stone which was an admission pass to the winner's celebration afterwards. This may picture the moment when the over comer will receive his ticket to the eternal victory celebration in heaven. The stone serves as a preview of the real thing to come as we march on as soldiers of the Lord. The words I heard on the beach resounded in my ears, don't give up; you're almost at the point of celebration! So I found some stones to take home. By the way, the stones raised questions from the airline attendants as they went through my suitcase!

Later, during my time alone in my room before retiring, I came to the passage in **Deuteronomy 1:31 (NKJV), "---The LORD your God carried you, as a man carries his son, in all the way that you went until you came to this place."** I wanted to shout to the heavens! He is amazing isn't He? What encouragement for this weary soul. Another passage was, **"No one engaged in warfare entangles himself with the affairs of this life, that he may please him who enlisted him as a soldier" 2 Timothy 2:4 (NKJV).**

I was also reading in the book I had taken along on the trip entitled, <u>Hinds Feet on High Places</u> by Hannah Hurnard just at this time and this is what it said: "My Lord, behold me—here I am, in the place Thou didst send me to---doing the thing Thou didst tell me to do....[1] Wow! Praise Him.

Satan's darts began to make me feel guilty for sitting on the patio alone with the Lord. The enemy suggested I go down to the motel to assist with some of the physical chores that needed to be done, anything to keep me from my quiet time. But as I turned the leaves of my Bible, my eyes fell on this passage, "Come aside by yourselves to a deserted place and rest awhile." Time was needed for rest and renewal. Vance Havner said it best, "If Christians do not come apart and rest awhile, they may just plain come apart!" We need to get refueled with our spiritual food just like we do when our physical bodies need nourishment. If not, then we are so tired and empty we are of no use to anyone.

I had signed up to help in the book store and be on the prayer team. After all I love books, and I love to pray for others. It started out the first day as planned, but God was soon to change those plans as He so often does. I was enjoying working at the bookstore. We had set up a display of items available at remarkably reasonable prices for the folks to purchase and take back with them. It was neat to see them getting Bible study workbooks so they could be encouraged in their walk and to assist them with teaching those folks in their respective places of service. One little girl came up and wanted a Bible because she had lost hers, and it was not easy for her to get one in her country. It thrilled my soul to be able to help her get just the one she wanted.

Each of the workers had to sign up to babysit one night while there, and I decided to sign up for the first night while a memorial service was going on. The two children of one couple were killed in an accident at an intersection as they were stopped waiting to pass through. How devastating! The emptiness and sorrow in the face of that mother will be indelibly imprinted on my mind forever. I cannot even imagine her loss. Some things we can't even pretend to understand. We must trust because we know His ways are not our ways.

I babysat Ezekiel and little Koen, a mongoloid baby, that night. As I had prayer- walked that very day I saw children by the names of Noah, Esther, Mary, Daniel, Joshua, Caleb, and etc. It was so amazing to see mostly biblical names that had been given to each one.

That night as I retired to my room the devotional scripture was in **John 13:14-15 (NKJV), "If I then, your Lord and Teacher have washed your feet, you also ought to wash one another's feet. For I have given you an example that you should do as I have done to you."** Our group definitely washed the feet of the people as we babysat, taught the children, gave haircuts, and provided other pampering gifts of service. We also prayed with and for the ones who had written their requests down for us.

God changed my direction of service as the medical leader asked me to assist with the health care needs. The doctor named it the Jubilee Crude (our theme for the program was Jubilee). It was a virus that attacked groups of folks each day. We set up clinic in one of the motel rooms on a hallway with no guests. We brought some medications from the states but found we needed many more. Each day a run was made to the local pharmacy to obtain more medicine which of course, was labeled in the language of the country. It made it a little more challenging to administer the proper drugs. I thought, "If joint commission could see me now!"

Many of the people had dealt with some of their physical ailments for months since medical care was hard to receive in their remote areas of service. I discovered that God had a plan and purpose in a few of the medicines we brought as we wondered how they would be used. After all, He is Jehovah Jireh, the provider.

We saw folks with coughs, colds, ear problems, athlete's feet, rashes, seizures, and even a baby who fell out of the swing and hurt his legs while playing. Some were sent to the hospital for treatment and evaluation. Little baby Koen had to be checked several times to guard against any respiratory problems.

On recognition night some of our friends' received 25-30 years of service to the Lord. How utterly amazing! They appeared to serve with little complaint and a whole lot of satisfaction. Forgive me, Lord, when I complain about anything. These folks have sacrificed their lives and contact with their families sometimes for years. Talking about denying yourself and taking up your cross!

My friend, Nora, and I were eating breakfast in preparation for one day. We had prayed that God would make us attentive to His divine appointments and in walked Jim, a fellow worker, who sat down to share with us. We each began sharing our prodigal son issues and cried and prayed over them all. We vowed to uplift each other in the days ahead. It was amazing to go that far across the water and connect with someone going through some of the same heartache. That was definitely a God thing.

That night a man by the name of Sam, shared his testimony about eight young men who years ago came to him in Vietnam. These men were uneducated, and they stole from him and each other. One man in particular gave him a run for his money, and he honestly thought none of them would amount to much with the attitudes they had. Several years later he went back to the area, and a man wanted him to come to a secluded area with him. He said he felt the peace of God to go. As he stepped into a clearing, out stepped the same young men with testimonies of how God was using them due to his witness. His message was, "Don't ever give up." That one you may think will never make it might just be the one God uses in a mighty way to bring others to Himself. Praise the Lord! What an encouragement to me! It served as another reminder to never give up on our prodigals.

Prayer: Thank you again, Father, for the opportunity to join You in what You are doing around the world. You have endeared my heart to so many who serve You on the mission field at such a great sacrifice to comfort, physical health, separation from family, and safety in some instances. However they have such peace and joy as they serve You in places You have called them. Remind me to keep them lifted up in prayer to You. Thank You that they are spreading the Word to many dark areas of the world. Place Your protection over them as they serve, Amen.

CHAPTER NINETEEN

Still On Our Knees

"Pray without ceasing." I Thessalonians 5:17, (NKJV).

It is evident as I return from my trip that Rob will be returning to prison, except by the grace of God. He has violated his probation and has a warrant out for his arrest. We are back to the days of expecting the law at our door. I continue to pray that God will stop his self-destruction and protect him wherever he is.

A friend whose son is also a prodigal allowed me to read a portion from the ebook, Setting Captives Free, Praying for the Unsaved by Jennifer Kennedy Dean. It reads as follows:

"How does the power of God impact a lost person's free will? Quote from S.D. Gordon's book:

> 'Quiet talks on prayer: The purpose of our praying is not to force or coerce his will, never that. It is to free his will of the warping influences that now twist it away. It is to get the dust out of his eyes so his sight shall be clear.

And once he is free, able to see aright, to balance things without prejudice the whole probability is in favor of his using his will to choose the only right.

I want to suggest to you the ideal prayer of such a one. It is an adaptation of Jesus own words. It may be pleaded with much vanity of detail. It is this:

Deliver him from the evil one; work in him Thy will for him by Thy power to Thy glory in Jesus, the Victors name...... The word "deliver" in this prayer as used by Jesus, the word under our English, has a picturesque meaning. It means rescue.

Here is a man taken captive and in chains. But he has become infatuated with his captor, and is befooled, regarding his condition.

Our prayer is "rescue" him from the evil one and because Jesus is Victor over the captor, the rescue will take place...... The prayer in Jesus name drives the enemy off the battlefield of the man's will and leaves him free to choose aright'."

Our prayers are like bombs falling on the enemies' strongholds and fortresses. Once we have destroyed his strongholds, his captives will be exposed to the light of the knowledge of God in the face of Christ, taken from II Corinthians 4:5.

Our prayers, the weapons of our warfare have divine power. In the fifth chapter of Ephesians, Paul describes our spiritual enemy (vv. 11-12) and our spiritual armor (vv. 13-17). After telling us to put on each piece of armor, you would expect his next words to be, "And fight." But what are his next words? And pray.... Prayer defeats the enemy in the lives of lost people." So we pray!

More from Setting Captives Free:

The following passage is taken from <u>Live a Praying Life: Open Your Life to God's Power and Provision</u>:

> "Another thing we learned about for the first time during the Gulf War, the war with Iraq, was "smart bombs." These are computer-driven bombs that hit a precise target. These bombs don't land in the general area of the target; they actually go through a window or down an elevator shaft. They are exact.
>
> As Satan has occupied territory, he has built strongholds, or fortresses. He has built these fortresses out of arguments and pretentions that set themselves up against the knowledge of God. Think of your Spirit-directed prayers as "smart bombs" landing on enemy strongholds. Your persevering prayers are precisely and systematically destroying Satan's hold."[1]

Usually upon my return from a mountain top experience there are things at home to face which are not pleasant, and this is no exception. Melissa, our daughter, was in the hospital for a few hours with pain and contractures while I was gone. My Dad is having pain in his side of undetermined origin (which always brings to our mind his past struggle with lymphoma of the stomach), and Robbie is in full blown rebellion once again.

We received a call that Robbie has been arrested for probation violation. He goes before the judge tomorrow. Once again God, the ultimate judge, gives reprieve through the earthly judge. Robbie has a chance to make things right if he will come home where he will be on house arrest for at least six months.

While in jail Robbie called us and promised to come straight home upon his release. The clock ticks on and we hear nothing from him all weekend. He is suppose to check in with his assigned probation officer on Monday. We wait once again to hear what will happen. The odds are good that he won't check in.

My scripture this morning is **Mark 11:22 (AMP), "And Jesus replying said to them, Have faith in God (constantly)." Hebrews 12:6 (NKJV), "For whom the Lord loves He chastens, and scourges every son He receives."**

Psalm 27:3, 14 (NIV), "Though an army besiege me, my heart will not fear; though war break out against me; even then will I be confident. Wait for the Lord; be strong and take heart and wait for the Lord." In Your strength Lord I won't give up hope. I will wait on You expectantly.

So many thoughts going through my mind, and I know where they come from. The enemy appears victorious in Rob's situation. He appears to have won the battle. But my heart knows different as I cling to the promises of God in **II Corinthians 2:14a, "Now thanks be unto God, who always causes us to triumph in Christ..."**

Very often the enemy seems to triumph for a little while, and God lets it be so, but then He comes in and upsets the work of the enemy, overthrowing the apparent victory. There He gets a great deal larger victory than we would have known if He had not allowed the enemy to seemingly, triumph in the first place.

If there is a trial in your life today, do not own it as a defeat, but continue, by faith, to claim the victory through Him who is able to make you more than a conqueror, and a glorious victory will soon be apparent. Let us learn that in all the hard places God brings us into, He is making opportunities for us to exercise such faith in Him as will bring about blessed results and greatly glorify His name.

I have been reading in Daniel recently and was in Chapter 9 this morning. I am praying it for Rob and all the prodigals I know as follows: **"O Lord, the great and awesome God, who keeps his covenant of love with all who love him and obey his commands, we have sinned and done wrong. We have been wicked and have rebelled; we have turned away from your commands and laws. We have not listened to your servants the prophets, who spoke in your name to our kings, our princes and our fathers, and to all the people of the land.**

"Lord, you are righteous, but his day we are covered with shame—the men of Judah and people of Jerusalem and all Israel, both near and far, in all the countries where you have scattered us because of our unfaithfulness to you. O LORD, we and our kings, our princes and our fathers are covered with shame because we have sinned against against you. The Lord our God is merciful and forgiving, even though we have rebelled against him; we have not obeyed the LORD our God or kept the laws he gave us through his servants the prophets. All Israel has transgressed your law and turned away, refusing to obey you" (NIV).

Gabriel came to Daniel to say that the moment he began praying, a command was given. He told him God loved him very much.

I trust you Lord that in Your timing You will bring the prodigals home from the enemies camp. Thank you for hearing my prayer at the time I pray it. You have scattered them because they have sinned against You. I will continue to stand in the gap even though I don't like what I am seeing in my own son. Lord help me be patient as I wait on You to act.

I read in Jennifer Kennedy Deans book, <u>Legacy of Prayer</u> the following:

"In praying for our children, our grandchildren, and our descendants, we must learn to pray in the Spirit and not in the flesh. Our mother-flesh and father-flesh is protective and possessive. The love we have for our children, in its flesh form, would like to control their lives and keep them from any pain, disappointment, or discouragement. Our flesh wants to rescue them and shield them and run interference for them. Our flesh will pray, "Don't let anything bad happen." To which the Lord will say, "I need to allow disappointment, pain, and failure so that I can give him the treasures of darkness and the riches stored in secret places."

As we pray for our children, we must die to our flesh connection with them and remain alive to the spiritual promise in them. Consider the story of Abraham, when God called on him to place Isaac on the altar.

To see this principle, we need to look at the account in the book of Genesis and the commentary on the story in the book of Hebrews.

The story begins, "God tested Abraham. He said to him. 'Abraham!' 'Here I am', he replied. Then God said, 'Take your son, your only son Isaac, whom you love, and go to the region of Moriah. Sacrifice him there as a burnt offering on one of the mountains I will tell you about.' Early the next morning, Abraham got up and saddled his donkey" (Genesis 22:1-3).

God tested Abraham. The word *test* is better translated, "proved". When God tests He is not trying to discover what is inside us. He is bringing what is inside to the outside. Don't think of this as a "trick" on Gods part. He is proving to Abraham what God knows is in him.

Abraham was connected to Isaac in two ways: First, Isaac was the son of his flesh. He was to Abraham "your son, your only son, Isaac, whom you love." (Genesis 22:2). You can imagine how very strong that connection was. After having waited and yearned for his son until all rational hope was gone and his and Sarah's bodies were long past childbearing years, at last Isaac was born. As his son, in the days of Abraham, Isaac was his property. He had the right to do with him as he chose. You know that every choice Abraham made concerning Isaac was made out of an overflow of love.

Abraham was connected to Isaac in another way. Isaac was also the child of promise, born by the power of the Spirit. (Galatians 4:28-29.) It was through Isaac, that all promise of God----that which had defined Abraham's entire adult life------was to be realized. "He who had received the promises was about to sacrifice his one and only son, *even though God had said to him*, 'It is through Isaac that your offspring will be reckoned' (Hebrews 11:17-19, emphasis added).

In requiring Abraham to die to his flesh connection, God did not require Abraham to die to the spiritual promise. Abraham, I believe, was more alive than ever to the promise in Isaac. As he reached the place of the sacrifice, "he said to his servants, 'Stay here with the donkey while I and the boy go over there. *We will worship* and then *we will come back to you*' (Genesis 22:5, emphasis added). By the time he had become fully yielded to the voice of God, by the time he had dealt the death blow to his own flesh, he had reached a new level of faith in God. He was absolutely certain that, no matter what path the promise took, the promise of God would not fail.

Abraham had already seen God bring life out of death. "Against all hope, Abraham in hope believed and so became the father of many nations, just as it had been said to him, 'So shall your offspring be.' Without weakening in his faith, he faced the fact that *His body was as good as dead*—since he was about a hundred years old—and that *Sarah's womb was also dead.* Yet he did not waver through unbelief regarding the promise of God, but was strengthened in his faith and gave glory to God, being fully persuaded that God had power to do what he had promised. (Romans 4:18-21, emphasis added). From Abraham's dead loins and Sarah's dead womb, Isaac was born. Isaac *was* a resurrection.

God is calling you with the same call Abraham heard "Take your son, your daughter, your granddaughter, and place him or her on My altar. Relinquish ownership. Die to your flesh connection, but remain alive to My promise. Your third day will come. You will look at this one and say, here is a resurrection.' "

Some of you are praying for children and grandchildren who are not saved or who are living in rebellion against God. Maybe you have been praying long enough that you are having a hard time holding on to hope. If you are the grandparent, then your pain is doubled because you are also feeling your child's pain. May the God of Abraham place His strong and loving arms around you right this minute as He assures you that He is the One "who gives life to the dead and calls into being that which does not exist" (Romans 4:17 NASB). He is the One who has the power to do what He has promised (Romans 4:21).

My dear friend, let me talk to you gently for a moment about the flesh that must go on the altar. Flesh doesn't like to die, and will put up quite a fight. Flesh will justify itself and argue for its life. So listen to the God of Abraham, not to your flesh.

Do you see any pride involved? Is part of your struggle that you are embarrassed? Do you wonder, just a little bit, if people might think you are a bad parent?

Is there some element of a desire to be in control mixed with your concern for your child? Are you frustrated that you can't make things happen the way you want them to? Might you need to take your flesh that needs to be in control and put it on the altar?

When the battle is tough, stand firm. When everyone else has left the battlefield, hold your ground. You are an Eleazar,

"Then the men of Israel retreated, but he (Eleazar) stood his ground and struck down the Philistines till his hand grew tired and froze to the sword. The Lord brought about a great victory that day." II Samuel 23: 9-10.

Like Eleazar, hold so tightly to your sword, that it hurts to hang on. Become one with your sword---"the sword of the Spirit, which is the Word of God." Ephesians 6:17.

Has the hand that holds your sword grown tired? Strike one more time. Has everyone else called the situation hopeless? Stand your ground. The Lord will give a great victory.

"When the Philistines banded together at a place where there was a field of lentils, Israel's troops fled from them. But Shamaiah took his stand in the middle of the field. He defended it and struck the Philistines down, and the Lord brought about a great victory." II Samuel 23:11-12.

Take your stand in the very center of the battle. Your victory is sure. Don't flee the battlefield when the warfare is fierce. You are the sure victor."[2]
Man, did you need to hear that the way I did? How powerful!

Sitting on my shelf is Henry Blackaby's book, <u>Created to be God's Friend</u>. I opened it tonight and a bookmark fell out from this page.

"Abraham's friendship with God was greater than his intense love for his only son, Issac. It had to be this way with God. There could be no competition in Abraham's heart, not even his dearest and most prized possession, his son!

Pure love for and trust in God were the only faith acceptable to God! For this faith God would grant righteousness in exchange. The relationship was completed with God in this act of ultimate sacrifice in obedience!"[3]

Man, I really needed to hear these words. God is preparing me. Am I willing to let him do the work needed to draw Rob to Himself. I must get out of the way.

I got a call before leaving for work that Rob had been arrested while at a friend's house last night. This "friend" that he has taken up with is all upset and says she is trying to get up enough money to get him out. I told her not to. He was where he needed to be. She hung up and I never heard from her again, but she did get him out. This was another area where Rob was totally blind. He had never stooped quite so low in his pursuits. It showed me where he was in his walk away from God. His stay inside was short this time.

My devotional this morning is in **Hebrews 5:8 (NKJV), "Though He was a Son yet he learned obedience by the things which He suffered."** My prayer is that Rob will also learn by the things he is suffering.

Little Brett, our first grandson, is due to arrive today and my scripture this morning says, "Adam (Bryan, our son-in-law), begat a son in his own image." How appropriate for the day. Melissa was quite a trooper and delivered naturally a big healthy baby boy. Anyone who sees the marvelous birth of a baby and does not believe in a Creator God needs their head examined. What a privilege to witness the birth of our first grandson. I do not take this privilege for granted. It is interesting that as the Father removes our son once again He gives us the gift of a little one to help fill that void. God is amazing.

Prayer: Lord, thank you for your reminder that You are the Victor. It may appear the enemy is winning, but we know who our Commander-in Chief is. Help us be more than conquerors. Remind us to pray for our prodigal's in the Spirit, and not in the flesh, Amen.

CHAPTER TWENTY

Yet Another Arrest

"And blessed is he, whosoever shall not be offended in Me" Matthew 11:6, (KJV).

Once again I got a call at work that Rob had been arrested. Apparently he is very high on drugs and was resisting arrest. I was told it took several officers' to control him. He is telling the officer that someone is trying to frame him with murder. The M word is all I heard. I was in total shock. I remember walking over to try to talk to my boss about the situation, and when she was not in her office walking back, but it was like I was in an out of body experience. I was in a world of my own, living out a total nightmare.

As I walked back in our area, someone asked me what was wrong and I felt like my legs were buckling under me. I kept asking God why He would allow this. If He had just kept him behind bars this would not have happened. I was in anguish.

There were three friends talking with me in our break room and they were trying to encourage me as I vented. It reminded me of Job's three friends, but his were accusing him of having sin in his life, mine were grieving with me and trying to encourage me, mostly just listening. I knew

God was trying to console me through the words of these friends as they allowed me to pour out my heart.

As I arrived home the phone rang. It was the arresting officer telling me Rob was in the hospital. Mother and Daddy came over and drove me to the hospital to see him. He had been beaten up pretty badly by the police. Rob said they had pinned him down and he felt he was literally smothering so he had come up fighting.

It was so hard to see him lying on the stretcher tied down with leather wrist and ankle restraints. He had bruises and abrasions all over him. The medical personnel talked about keeping him overnight, but decided that he could go home. If we had not been there to take him I don't know what would have happened to him.

I got in the bed at 1:30 a.m. and had to get up to go to work at 5:30 a.m. the next morning. Needless to say it was a short night. I just kept repeating, I can do all things through Christ Who strengthens me, to myself. In my quiet time I came to **Philippians 4:19 (NAS), "And my God shall supply all your needs according to His riches in glory by Christ Jesus."**

For Rob I had **Hosea 11:10 (TLB), "For the people shall walk after the Lord. I shall roar as a lion (at their enemies) and My people shall return trembling from the west. Like a flock of birds they will come from Egypt---like doves flying from Assyria. And I will bring them home again; it is a promise from the Lord."**

In Hebrews 6:18 (TLB), "He has given both His promise and His oath, two things we can completely count on, for it is impossible for Him to tell a lie."

I think my coworkers were quite surprised to see me come in the next day. The Lord and I have come a long way together. He gave me peace and calm in the midst of the storm. Just His presence within me helps to calm the storm raging on the external.

The panic Rob had of someone setting him up with murder was false. I don't know if the drugs had him in that state, but I know one thing, he was scared and as he said, running for his life. I know the enemy used it to distress and worry me but God used it for Rob's good. God got him away from the horrible influences of so called friends and put him in a place of protection in answer to our prayers. Otherwise I believe he would have been dead from the drugs.

My Dad and I had to take Rob down to the magistrate's office because his probation officer had called to say they had a warrant for him for violation of probation. Rob kept asking if he would have to stay. I talked with Jimmy and we really felt he would be better coming home for the night so we could talk and spend some time with him before his court date but decided not to put the bond money down for his release.

Tough love was certainly named right. It is so hard to see him go into the room with the lady knowing he will be behind bars for some time to come.

I often go to my car during my lunch break to eat and have some moments of quiet and renewal. That day I had the workbook, "Believing God", by Beth Moore and I opened to the page that talked about the unoffended being blessed. **"And blessed is he, whosoever shall not be offended in Me." Matthew 11:6 (KJV).**

Beth wrote, "I'd go so far as to suggest that the deeper we have loved God, the deeper the potential for devastation when He doesn't intervene as we know He can." How true. It is not a problem of believing He can work and intervene in Rob's life it is "when Lord", that drives me crazy some days.

Beth also wrote, "Blessed are we when we could be offended and choose with every shred of tattered faith not to be."[1] I know God was asking me not to be offended with Him in this matter and I like Shadrach, Meshach and Abednego chose to trust and believe Him regardless whether he rescues me from this fiery furnace.

Romans 8:31b (NIV), "If God is for me, who can be against me." Who can be our foe if God is on our side? Psalm 118:6 (AMP), "The Lord is on my side. I will not fear. What can man do to me?" Hebrews 13:6 (AMP), "The Lord is my helper. I will not be seized with alarm. I will not fear or dread or be terrified. What can man do to me?"

The court case was today and Rob was sentenced to 56 months. His grandparents were there, since Jimmy and I are working, and they had an opportunity to speak a word in his behalf to the judge. It is so hard for his family to hear but we had tried to brace ourselves for the worse.

We had all certainly hoped that we would not have to go back to visit our son in prison. It is so hard to have to explain to his daughters, Carolyn and Shelbi. They love him so much, and of course we will take them to see him. They ask about him often and wonder where he is. Oh Lord, it is so hard some days, but we trust You as the final judge.

The first time I went to see Rob he told me, "I have come out of the darkness." I came to the scripture in **Ephesians 5: 8, 11 (AMP), "For once you were darkness, but now you are light in the Lord; walk as children of light---lead the lives of those native-born to the Light. Take no part in and have no fellowship with the fruitless deeds and enterprises of darkness, but instead (let your lives be so in contrast as to) expose and reprove and convict them."**

He has certainly come out of the darkness of the world he found himself involved in, using cocaine. No matter how many times we face this process it is so painful and we know we have lost so much valuable time with our son. God reminded me not long ago that I will have time with him for eternity since we believe he is a child of God and has accepted Christ. Praise the Lord! What a comfort. Is his ministry and turn around going to come even as he is in that prison cell? Lord teach him, speak to him, change his heart and mind towards the things of Your dear self. Make him to shine in that place because he has been with you, the Light of the world.

There are so many within those walls that need you. I pray that the chains the enemy has placed on each one of them will be loosed and that You Father have come to set the prisoners free.

You know we can be in chains and shackles even though we may not be behind physical bars. We are captive to gossip, knowledge, tobacco, drugs and alcohol, fear, pride in what we have and in what we can do in life, and our own view of our self-worth. We condemn the prisoner for their actions but we murder people's characters with our lips while building ourselves up. We may even rob the Lord by withholding our tithes and offerings or our government by cheating on our taxes, etc.

I don't know about you but I find I cannot throw the stone at another when I do self-examination and find myself so lacking. Let's not throw the stones at our fellow brother or sister in Christ or the lost as the people did Stephen. As Stephen died he was asking the Father to forgive the people because they did not know what they were doing. Oh that I would be that gracious when others throw their stones of condemnation at me.

Melissa, Brett and I were at the beach for a short time away and I was very down one day. I told Melissa I was going for a walk and took my CD player to listen to as I walked. I cried and sang praises to the Lord and felt my spirits lifting.

As I walked I got over in the soft sand and began to sink down so I knew I needed to step over to a more solid ground. About that time the song rang in my ears, "Solid Rock." My hope is built on nothing less than Jesus blood and righteousness. I dare not trust the sweetest frame but wholly lean on Jesus name. On Christ the solid rock I stand, all other ground is sinking sand. All other ground is sinking sand.

It was amazing encouragement to me. God is so faithful to give us a word if we are listening. He is always meeting our needs and bringing hope to our spirit. I don't want to miss a single word He has for me, how about you?

As I had my time with the Lord this morning I read from my Charles Spurgeon devotion book:

> "Sitting at a table once I heard a Mother speaking at length about her son. She said a very great deal about him. Then someone sitting near me said, "I wish that good woman would be quiet." But I said, "What is the matter? May she not speak of her son? He said, "Why he has been deported. He was as bad a fellow as ever lived, and yet she always sees something wonderful in him."
>
> So some time later when I gained her acquaintance I ventured to say something to her about this son. I remember her remark, "If there is nobody else to speak up for him, then his Mother will." She loved him so that if she could not be altogether blind to his faults, yet she would also see all that was hopeful in him." [2] I know this Mothers heart.

We received a letter from Rob and I wanted to insert it here:

"I'm in the last week of Dart (his drug program). I have learned a lot with other people sharing their drug history and how crack has ruined their lives. I can relate very well. Crack has and is ruining lives. I'm so afraid of what this drug is doing to the world. It makes you feel so good and at the same time that's all you focus on. You take everything for granted and treat people like nothing.

You have no words and when you run out of crack, you're the devil. You don't care about yourself so how in the world can you care about anyone else.

I've stayed awake for days at a time sometimes seven to nine without sleep. I've spent days without showers, without eating. Now that I look back what a way to live, huh? All I used to think about was the next hit, anything else didn't matter. I didn't care who I hurt, cause deep down inside I was hurting. I felt hopeless, I felt guilty, I felt ashamed. I felt angry until the point I felt nothing!

I would keep telling myself after this bag I'm done, after this hit I'm done but when it was gone all I thought about was more, more, more. I'm lucky to be alive right now; when I was smoking I didn't care. I really thought I was the Hulk when I was smoking. I'm unstoppable. That's what I thought. It gave me power, I thought.

I love you guys so much, I never meant to hurt you, I'm sorry. Thank God I have you for my parents. I truly mean that. Don't you ever think it was your fault. It was mine. I love you." Rob.

I cherish his writings. As you can tell he is aware what it does to you when he is away from it but when he is so into it you can't reason with him. He is blinded by the wiles of the devil.

If you find yourself in the strongholds of the enemy whether in drugs or alcohol or sexual addiction I beg you to listen to the words of this letter. Don't wait till you are forced to come to your senses in prison or an accident or some other painful experience to wake up to the realization that the devil has deceived you all along. There is only one way freedom will come and that is through Christ. He sets the captive free and then he shall be free in deed.

We have a long way to go but I know God is working in Rob's life and in His timing he will totally surrender his life to his Heavenly Father. He is reading (which is a miracle within itself) testimonies of others and "The Purpose Driven Life."

So many of our Bible Study Fellowship friends and other close friends have been so faithful to correspond with him and send him books. It reminds me of the passage in **Matthew 25:36 (AMP), "I was naked and you clothed Me; I was sick and you visited Me with help and ministering care; I was in prison and you came to see Me."**

In Isaiah 58:7b (NIV), "......not to turn away from your own flesh and blood?" God will bless you for your ministry to the one held captive. But by the grace of God, there go you and I.

Rob appealed his case and actually won with the help of an inmate who knew the law. He was able to come out 2 years earlier than anticipated. This could have only been God.

He is now reunited with Tina (though still unmarried) and they are now expecting a third child, who they named Kane. Rob has had a lot of hard knocks since his release but I can see God working in them all. God has certainly shown me that the things I thought were horrid were all working for Rob's good. It might not have looked good at the time, but God worked them all out for good. He had to get his attention in some areas and He certainly has done a work in his whole little family.

I don't know what other chapters God will add to my life but I know I can trust Him with whatever comes my way. He holds my hand through each experience and helps me to endure till He comes to receive me unto Himself. My eyes are anxiously looking for the first sight of His marvelous face. In the meantime, I must be about my Father's business.

> *Prayer: Lord, may I never be offended with You when things do not go in the way I would like. Help me to chose with every shred of tattered faith I have not to be angry with You. Help me to trust in You as I may find myself in the furnace of affliction, believing with my whole heart that You are with me even there, Amen.*

CHAPTER TWENTY-ONE

Suicide Attempt

"For You have delivered my life from death, yes, and my feet from falling, that I may walk before God in the light of life and of the living" Psalm 56:13, (AMP).

It seems that each time we attempt to get out of town for some rest and relaxation things develop with our son in such a way that we find ourselves coming back home before our time is up. This year was no exception. We had been relaxing at a friend's beautiful beach house taking long walks on the beach, cooking wonderful seafood at night, resting and relaxing with no agenda. Early on Friday morning, I was awakened with a call from our daughter, Melissa, saying that our son was in the hospital due to a suicide attempt.

The morning before God had taken me to II Chronicles 20 (AMP) to write for our loved ones newsletter, but as I look back on it, it was really meant for our family for this new crisis. Needless to say we began to pack and clean up for the long journey home, and once again the vacation was over.

Jehoshaphat had a great multitude coming against him. In v.3, "Then Jehoshaphat feared, and set himself [determinedly, as his vital need] to seek the Lord and proclaimed a fast in all Judah". He acknowledged who God was, powerful and mighty. He was someone who no one could withstand. He cried to God in his affliction, and God promised to hear and save him. Are you crying out to Him in your pain and the loss of your hopes for the future?

In **verse 12, "O our God, will You not exercise judgment upon them? For we have no might to stand against this great company that is coming against us. We do not know what to do, but our eyes are upon You."** As loved ones I am sure you, like me, have often not known what to do in the situation you find yourself in. In this verse we are admonished to keep our eyes on God. Where are your eyes, on God and what He is doing or on the enemy? We are in a spiritual battle for our prodigals for sure, but God promises to take care of the enemy, we just need to keep our focus on Him.

In **verse 15b** He instructs us, **"Be not afraid or dismayed at this great multitude; for the battle is not yours but God's."** Is that as comforting to you as it is to me? The battle is not ours. I have to be reminded of that so often because I go back to thinking it is my battle and I am in control. Letting go and letting God is a battle I fight every day. A controller wants to be in control not only of their situation, but the other person. That's me. I want so much for my son to be all he can be in the Lord's army and I have often tried to manipulate things in his life. I struggle with that daily. God reminds me in His Word, as I seek after Him, that there is One and only One in control, and it isn't me!

Our daughter explains that she had gotten a call in the wee hours of the morning from our son's fiancée, Tina, saying that Rob had called her saying he had taken a handful of Benadryl and other substances and didn't want to live anymore. Melissa called our house and talked to Rob telling him she was on her way over. She then called my Dad, who met her at our house not knowing what they would encounter in the wee hours of the morning.

When they arrived at our home Rob had left. He had driven about 15 miles from our home to the home he had been living in with Tina, by the grace of God he arrived safely. Not knowing where he might have gone Melissa and my Dad drove over to that house and found him with the front door unlocked already in a stupor and foaming at the mouth. They immediately called 911 and the emergency crews took him to the hospital after pumping his stomach. If you don't see God in all of that I don't know why not. Rob should have been dead so many times with drug addiction and accidents but God continues to spare his life.

In **verse 17** He reminds us**: "You shall not need to fight in this battle: Take your position, stand still, and see the deliverance of the LORD [who is] with you, O Loved one. Fear not, nor be dismayed; tomorrow go out against them, for the LORD is with you."** We can go out in prayer against the enemy who seeks to kill and destroy our prodigal's. Often I hear folks say, "All we can do is pray". That is our greatest privilege, to pray. That is to be our position, like in **verse 18, "Jehoshaphat bowed his head with his face to the ground, and fell down before the LORD, worshipping Him."**

In **verse 19, "and they stood to praise the LORD GOD of Israel with a loud voice."** When is the last time you praised the Father. Sometimes days can run into each other while we wallow in our misery of the moment and we forget to sing praise to our Lord. The enemy can come in with a vengeance with his fiery darts aimed at our emotions. He can convince us of anything, but as we praise our Lord he has to flee. I find when I am so down I can put in those praise CD's and singing along with them begins to lift my spirits.

In **verses 22-23, "And when they began to sing and to praise the LORD set ambushments against the men of Ammon, Moab, and Mount Seir, who had come against Judah, and they were [self] slaughtered; For [suspecting betrayal] the men of Ammon and Moab rose against those of Mt. Seir, utterly destroying them. And when they had made an end of the men of Seir, they all helped to destroy one another."** Are you convicted that you have neglected to praise the Father in spite of your circumstances? That is when He destroys the enemy.

In the midst of our trial as we returned home I kept repeating, "The battle is Yours Lord, it is not mine". Just having that fresh word in my mind got me through some difficult days to come. God had prepared me for this battle and He did bring deliverance for our son. We praise Him for what He did through the incident. I beg you to stay in His Word daily because He may just be preparing you for the battle of your life. You need His instructions and the assurance He is with you through it. Knowing that, you will be able to do all things through Him who gives you strength.

Some are chosen to remain in affliction even to the point of martyrdom in the highest call of suffering. We each have our own crosses, but some of lesser degrees it seems. God does not allow us to be tempted above that which we are able to bear. Some of us have questioned that at times in our lives as the tests presented themselves.

What good does it do to keep to ourselves how God has brought us through the difficulties? It is difficult to be open with others about the struggles we have walked through, but to whom do you want to talk when you have been or are going through some difficult situation in life? Isn't it someone who understands your pain, having walked a similar path before you? Someone who came through, bearing testimony of God's faithfulness to see them through?

I would like to share with you something from the devotional of C. H. Spurgeon which I read from almost daily:

The scripture is **Psalm 42:7a (NIV),"Deep calls to deep..."**

> "Great depths of trial bring with them great depths of promise. For you, much afflicted one, there are great and mighty words which are not meant for others of easier experience. You shall drink from deep goblets of truth that are reserved for the giants of faith, men of capacity enough to quaff deep draughts of the well-refined words of God. Trials are mighty enlargers to the soul. We are normally contracted, narrowed, pent up, and can rightly pray, "Lord, enlarge my heart." Yes, but the opening of capacious reservoirs within us can only be affected by the spade of deep, daily tribulation. Then, having been dug out by pain and trouble, room is created in us for the overflowing promises of God. A great adversity will bring great grace to the believer. Whenever the Lord sets His servants to do extraordinary work, then He always gives them extraordinary strength---and He puts them to unusual suffering, giving them unusual patience (as He did Paul).
>
> If God calls you to common and ordinary trials, He will pay the charges of your warfare by thousands. But if He commands you to an unusual struggle with tremendous foe, than He will discharge the liabilities of that war by millions, according to the riches of His grace in which He has abounded toward us through Christ Jesus. In your better mind, would you want to escape great labors or great trials, since in them are promised to you great graces?"[1]

We must learn that having joy is not going to mean we experience happiness each day. There have been many, many days I have not been happy about what was going on but found I could have the joy of the Lord and peace that comes only from Him even in the midst of the pain. There is nothing like His peace!

I've read this verse many times, **"For the eyes of the Lord run to and fro throughout the whole earth, to show Himself strong on behalf of those whose heart is loyal to Him" II Chronicles 16:9 (NKJV).** I want to be found loyal and righteous like Abraham, a friend such as David, bold for Christ like Paul, a rock like Peter, as obedient as Moses was, blameless and upright, and a woman who fears God and shuns evil much like Job. I don't know what you are facing this moment in your life, but I do know you can persevere if you are leaning on Jesus and stay in God's Word which is alive and active.

Table of Grace sung by Phillips, Craig and Dean, has ministered to me so much as I think of those in darkness being welcomed to the table of grace. It is taken from Matthew 11:28-30 and reads as follows:

Table of Grace

"Hear the good news
You've been invited
No matter what others may say
Your darkest sins will be forgiven
And you will always have a place.
At the table of grace
The cup's never empty
The plates always full
And it's never too late
To come and be filled
With love never ending
You're always welcome at the table of grace.
So come you weak and heavy hearted
Don't try to hide your earthly scars
In His eyes we all are equal
Don't be afraid, come as you are
So let the first become the last
Let the poor put kings to shame
Their hearts will be their treasure
By the power of Jesus name
Everyone's welcome at the table of grace."[2]

Hallelujah! What an awesome invitational song. If you don't know Jesus, come and be filled with His life everlasting right now. That is my cry for each of you. If you haven't already come to His table of grace won't you come right now? He is waiting for you with arms outstretched no matter what you have done.

> *Prayer: Thank you so much Lord for the journey we have been on. I, like Much Afraid, have had to walk a hard journey, but I wouldn't have missed it for all the gold in the world. Thank You for inviting me into Your very chambers. Thank You for teaching me to hear Your voice and obey Your instructions. Thank You Lord that I KNOW You love me. Thank You for allowing me to see Your grace and mercy and teaching me to demonstrate the same to others. Thank You for how I am seeing You work in the hearts of our family to bring healing and restoration. I could go on and on but just know, I love You with all my heart and soul and mind! Amen.*

CHAPTER TWENTY-TWO

Birth of On Wings Like a Dove Ministry

"I said, "Oh, that I had wings like a dove! I would fly away and be at rest" Psalm 55:6, (NIV).

Lynda Randle sings a song that blesses my heart and helps me to remember that God is the same God when I am in the valley that He is on the mountain. The words go as follows, may it bless your heart:

GOD ON THE MOUNTAIN
by Tracy G. Dartt

"Life is easy when you're up on the mountain
And you've got peace of mind like you've never known
But when things change and you're down in the valley
Don't lose faith for you're never alone.

CHORUS:
And the God on the mountain is still God in the valley
When things go wrong He'll make them right
And the God of the good times is still God in the hard times
The God of the day is still God in the night

We talk of faith when we're up on the mountain
But talk comes easy when life's at its best
But in the valley of trials and temptations
That's when faith is really put to the test."[1]

Isn't that so true? As long as life is good and we are prosperous we seem to believe that God is good, but let the trials come and we find ourselves down in the valley. We lose sight of the fact that God remains the same faithful God. He never leaves us nor forsakes us but uses our circumstances to mold us, making us into vessels useful for His service.

I love to read Watchman Nee's writings and he writes about the breaking process in his book, The Release of the Spirit:

> "Since being saved, we have been touched many times in various ways by the Lord, all with the purpose of breaking our outward man. Whether we are conscious of it or not, the aim of the Lord is to break this outward man........What is the final objective of the Lord's working in our lives? It is to break this earthen vessel, to break our alabaster box, to crack open our shell. The Lord longs to find a way to bless the world through those who belong to Him. Brokeness is the way of blessing, the way of fragrance, the way of fruitfulness, but it is also a path sprinkled with blood. Yes, there is blood from many wounds.......Each of us must find out for himself what is the mind of the Lord in his life. It is a most lamentable fact that many do not know what is the mind or intention of the Lord for their lives..... The Lord has not wasted even one thing. To understand the Lord's purpose, is to see very clearly that He is aiming at a single objective: the breaking of the outward man.
>
> However, too many, even before the Lord raises a hand, are already upset. Oh, we must realize that all the experiences, troubles and trials which the Lord sends us are for our highest good. We cannot expect the Lord to give better things, for these are His best. Should one approach the Lord and pray, saying, "O Lord, please let me choose the best," I believe He would tell them, "What I have given you is the best; your daily trials are for your

greatest profit." So the motive behind all the orderings of God is to break our outward man. Once this occurs and the spirit can come forth, we begin to be able to exercise our spirit." [2]

Are you willing to allow the Lord to break you so that you can be poured out with His sweet fragrance to be used in any way He sees fit? I am so glad He chose to break this vessel, even though the breaking has oftentimes been unpleasant. Many times we can't see His purpose during the breaking experience, but as we continue on the journey He shows us what He was up to. I thank Him for the season of breaking in our families lives!

His breaking in me has birthed a ministry to the loved ones of prodigals and prisoners. The name of it is On Wings Like a Dove, taken from **Psalm 55:6-8 (NIV), "O, that I had wings like a dove! For then would I fly away and be at rest—I would flee far away and stay in the desert, I would hurry to my place of shelter, far from the tempest and storm"**

Have you ever felt that way? I often wanted to fly away to that place of rest from the difficulties I was facing with our son. Looking back, I wouldn't take anything for the journey I have had with my Heavenly Father as He has done His work in me.

One day as I prayed, I was led to meet with one of our pastor's as I described my burden to minister to others walking through the pain of having a prodigal or loved one in prison. I felt that even the families in our church who were affected were not being ministered to, nor were their child or spouse who was incarcerated. I knew the shame of having that wayward child and feeling many Sundays as I entered the church like putting a bag over my head.

As we finished sharing, he gave me the name of a couple who were entering the hardships of an upcoming imprisonment and needed support. As I met with them we shared and I was able to go with them as the husband turned himself into federal prison. I was privileged to help his wife walk through the difficult days ahead of her over the year that followed. My husband and I also went to visit with the husband, and wrote to him with encouragement, spiritual mentoring and promises to pray.

That is when God began to show me that that was what He wanted to use me to do with other families going through the challenge their prodigal presented, whether that entailed prison or walking away from God's plan and purpose for their lives due to drugs or in other ways of disobedience.

Finally, I knew I was once again in His perfect will for my life. We now minister in one way or another to over forty families as God brings them across our path. It has been an amazing journey in which God has turned my pain into His glory.

We count it a privilege to bring these loved one's hope and encouragement. We teach them to take one day at a time, staying in the word of God, and standing in the gap for their loved one who can't for the moment. It is a spiritual battle worth fighting as we intercede for our family members and friends. The enemy wants nothing more than to discourage us, oppress us, and cause us to be useless in God's army, but God's intent is to strengthen us through the trial and use us to bring Him glory.

It is not easy reliving the pain as I listen to others share, but oh so worth it to see them come to grips with their pain and release it to God. Some are not willing to come to walk that healthy path to freedom from shame and sorrow, but we continue to reach out with the hope that they will one day enjoy their freedom in Christ as they release their loved one to the One in control. God does such a better job than I ever did as He teaches our son how He wants him to live his life.

What will you do with the pain you are experiencing? Will you allow God to use it for His kingdom purposes? I have seen crying, struggling Mother's over time learn to release their child to God and have seen them grow spiritually and emotionally, some even seeing their prodigal come back home.

I pray these few words will bless you which were taken from John MacArthur's book, A Tale of Two Sons:

> "When the father reached the wayward son, he couldn't contain his affection, and he didn't hesitate in granting forgiveness. This was even more shocking to the Pharisees than the imagery of a grown man sprinting down a dusty road to greet a derelict son.
>
> The father immediately embraced the Prodigal. Jesus said the father "fell on his neck and kissed him" (v. 20). The verb tense means he kissed him repeatedly. He collapsed on the boy in a massive hug, buried his head in the neck of his son—stinking and dirty and unpresentable as he was—and welcomed him with a display of unbridled emotion.

It is evident that the father had been suffering in quiet grief the entire time the boy was gone. His deep love for the youth had never once wavered. The yearning to see him wise up and come home must have been a painful burning in the father's heart. It filled his thoughts every day. And now that he saw the bedraggled figure of his son alone on the horizon, it mattered little to the father what people thought of him; he was determined to welcome home the boy as personally and publicly as possible.

Furthermore, the father would spare the boy from any more of the reproach of his sin—by becoming a reproach himself. In essence, he took the boy's disgrace completely upon himself—emptying himself of all pride, renouncing his fatherly rights, not caring at all about his own honor (even in that culture, where honor seemed like everything). And in an amazing display of selfless love—openly despising the shame of it all (cf. Hebrews 12:2)—he opened his arms to the returning sinner and hugged him tightly in an embrace designed partly to shield him from any more humiliation. By the time the boy walked into the village, he was already fully reconciled to his father.

The Prodigal had come home prepared to kiss his Father's feet. Instead, the father was kissing the Prodigal's pig-stinking head. Such an embrace with repeated kisses was a gesture that signified not only the father's delirious joy but also his full acceptance, friendship, love, forgiveness, restoration, and total reconciliation. It was a deliberate and demonstrative way of signaling to the whole village that the father had fully forgiven his son, without any qualms or hesitancy.

What a beautiful picture this is of the forgiveness offered in the gospel! The typical sinner wants out of the morass of sin, and his first instinct is to devise a plan. He will work off his guilt. He will reform himself. But such a plan could never succeed. The debt is too great to repay, and the sinner is helpless to change his own status. He is fallen, and he cannot alter that fact. So the Savior intercepts him.

Christ has already run the gauntlet, taken the shame for himself, suffered the rebukes, borne the cruel taunts, and paid the price of the guilt in full. He embraces the sinner, pours out love upon him, grants complete forgiveness, and reconciles him to God."[3]

Hallelujah! He has demonstrated an amazing display of grace to each of us when we were prodigals. How can we not love Him with all our hearts, and souls, and minds? God gave us the ultimate gift of forgiveness and accepted us back into the kingdom of God when we did not deserve it. Praise to our Heavenly Father. If you need to come home to the Father, do so today. He is waiting with open arms.

Some of my greatest moments in ministry have been as I sat with prodigals in a group setting and heard them share how God is restoring them. Coming out of addictions to drugs and alcohol is often difficult, but these men and women are discovering what it truly means to be free. They have been in bondage and captivity, oftentimes even though they were not in prison, because of the lies of the devil. I heard one man testify that he didn't even stop using drugs in prison. What greater joy than to see souls released from the enemies grip as they learn to rest in the arms of our dear Savior.

I saved a newsletter I received from Charles Stanley in 2002. I would like to share it with you here to encourage you if you find yourself in a trial:

"Oftentimes God will allow trials in our lives that are so imposing that we think He has either abandoned us or made a mistake. But God does not make mistakes. He allows affliction in our lives in order to push us ahead, strengthen us, and cause us to grow. These obstacles allow Him to demonstrate His faithfulness and the incredible capacity He has given us to rise above adversity.

Joshua is an awesome example of encouragement to those who face difficulty and hardship in life! If we, like Joshua, are to exercise courage in our obedience to God, we must face the challenges He sends or allows in our lives without fear and uncertainty in our spirits. God is our refuge and strength; He will take care of us regardless of the trials we encounter."[4]

I pray you will understand that God does not make mistakes, nor does He ever abandon us in our time of trial. He has a plan and a purpose in everything we face in life. May we all learn from our struggles to lean on our Heavenly Father. His arms are huge!

Our son is out of prison and slowly making his way back to the Father. Often times the prodigal doesn't come back the way we envision nor in the timing we set but I pray we will all accept however they choose to come and watch to see how God works in their lives with encouragement, not condemnation. Will you be grateful for the effort they are making to come back home, or will you criticize and judge them because it is not always to your liking? If they are headed back home, that is what matters, right? I know we could be one phone call away from a crisis again, but I chose to revel in what God is doing in our family as He has brought healing and restoration to us. We still have a long way to go but as I have heard Beth Moore say, "We aren't where we need to be, but praise God we aren't where we used to be".

Rob and Tina are back together and planning to be married in the future. They chose to have a son on his return home, whom they have named Kane. Here again, I find that I am not in control of their choices. Hopefully they will come to terms with God's perfect plan to bring their little family together as husband and wife in the near future. I am also praying for them to connect with a local church body and grow in the Lord together. I have turned this over to the Lord Who knows how to draw them to Himself.

I would like to share what my son recently texted me, that helped me know he is making his way back to the Father. It read as follows:

"Your words were gentle, so sweet and so kind, they will get me through the day and stay fresh on my mind. Thank you for loving me, I'm not blind anymore, God lets me see." Praise to the Lord. I framed this and hung it in our den to read often in reminder that our prodigal is beginning to see God's plan for his life. Persevere with faith loved one, believing God's promises to you for your prodigal. It may take years, but trust God to do what He says He will do. Abraham *believed* and it was accounted to him for righteousness. It took years for him to receive the promise of a son, but it did happen!

Our granddaughters have accepted the Lord into their hearts and were baptized this year. I am so glad I have been privileged to take them to the Lord's house. We pray that in due time Brett and Kane will also make that choice in their hearts which will complete our family circle.

I hope you can see where the Lord had this prodigal's mother. She was on her knees in prayer, in God's boot camp, being refined as silver, learning to trust the Lord, attempting to go about the will of the Father as He extended His call in everyday life, and remaining glued to His Word for encouragement and fulfillment of His promises to bring her prodigal home. You may not have seen the mother running down that path to greet the prodigal, but you can bet she was in the kitchen preparing the fatted calf!

I will end with the words my dear friend Joan always says, "And so we pray." Lord I do so hope I have been faithful to put down the words You would have me to. Help me accomplish the final click as it goes to press and trust You to do with it what you will. It's been quite an adventure with You and I love You so much.

> *Prayer: Lord, use our ministry to families of prodigals and prisoners to bring healing but more importantly, glory to You our Father. I love you Lord for choosing our family in the furnace of affliction. I pray You can see Your reflection more clearly. Continue to mold us and make us into vessels that are poured out to others, Amen.*

ON WINGS

On Wings Like a Dove we take flight
To spread a message of hope and light
For souls broken-hearted and imprisoned,
We are called to share a heavenly provision.

Surely we will find if we search our minds
A common bond with the prodigals we meet;
Were we not lost before we heard of the Cross,
Without direction like those wandering the street?

Lord, use us to tell about your infinite love,
To those separated and alone, away from the families they've known
As encouragers, help us give counseling and direction
Through God's Word many souls find eternal protection.

So spread your wings and soar
Lift up families who are hurting, comfort prisoners, the deserting,
Guide them to our open door,
Introduce the Christ…they are lost no more.

Sandy Pulliam 2008

ACKNOWLEDGEMENTS

My first appreciation is to my Heavenly Father Who has shown me His love by allowing me to remain in the crucible of pain and suffering in order to burn away the dross so I would become more and more like Him. Continue to do the work in me that needs to be done, Lord.

To my husband, Jimmy, who walked the journey with me not only with our prodigal, but through the tragic losses we experienced in our lives. He has always been supportive in what God has called me to do by allowing me the freedom to go in obedience. He has endured many days on his own as I got away to work on this project and in the ministry God led me to.

My children, Melissa and Rob, God used you to teach me so much along this journey of life. Melissa, I praise God that you bear no resemblance to the elder brother in the story of the Prodigal Son. You are merciful and gracious and have such a gentle, forgiving spirit. Thank you for always being there for your brother as he has poured out his struggles and sought your advice. Thank you for giving such loving support to your parents. I love you so much!

Rob, has asked me several times, "Mom, don't you wish you had never birthed me"? No! I shudder to think what I would have missed with my Heavenly Father. That was when God did His work in me to change a heart filled with judgmental attitudes, unforgiving attitudes, and works that were not pleasing to Him. I would have never realized that the Lord desires us to have a personal relationship with Him. Therefore I would have missed out on the most important relationship of my life. Thank you for what you have allowed me to learn. God continues to teach me through you. I love you for being honest enough to be yourself.

My parents, Jim and Anne Scales, have been such great influences in my walk with the Lord. They have interceded on our families' behalf day in and day out, and I want to thank them for their love, counsel, and support over the years. What would I have done without their shoulders to cry on, their wise counsel, and more importantly their constant prayers?

I want to thank Debbie Hampton, my best friend and adopted sister, who has listened to me cry, wail, express my anger, and hopelessness to her over the past twenty-five years. I thank her for her sweet prayers on behalf of our family and her unconditional love for me. What a gift God gave me in her friendship. She is to me as Jonathan was to David. She has given me far more than I have given her as she has walked quietly beside me. Thank you Debbie for encouraging me to do things I thought were impossible

Thank you to my dear friends, Cathy Hill, Cindy Miller, and Lynn Whitley. They have cried, laughed and prayed with me over the years, sometimes in tune with me because of their own prodigal children. I thank them for their commitment to pray and how God has used their prayers in ways they will never know. We have had a blast together as we have over and over seen God's hand move in each other's lives. You are all so dear and precious to me and my eyes fill up with tears, heartfelt love, and devotion to each of you as I ponder all our adventures together.

Thank you to my spiritual mother, Joan Long, who taught me so many truths of the Father as we knelt on our knees in prayer for seven wonderful years under our pastor's pulpit. We have gathered often since that time to develop a deep love for each other. The knowledge I had that she was in constant intercession for me has often kept me going beyond what I felt I could.

Dee Dee Harrison, Melinda Lawson, and Phyliss Huffman, who joined us in prayer and have continued to join together in prayer beyond that season we had together. They have each joined me in ministry to the loved one of prodigals/prisoners as God led them. I love each one of you.

I want to thank our pastor's and teacher's who helped me grow in my spiritual walk with God. Thank you for your counsel over the years and for your prayers. Thank you to our longtime pastor, Dr. Gary Chapman who took the time to read my manuscript and write the forward. He has been such a blessing in the life of our family. I still have a note from our beloved pastor, Dr. Mark Cort's telling me, "I pray for Rob often".

Hopefully as he walks those streets of gold he will know how much those words blessed this mother's heart.

I want to thank Frank and Cindy Miller, Henry and Nancy Williamson, Jayne Hillman, and Rocky Underwood for allowing me to retreat to their glorious homes on the lake and in the mountains to write. It gave me the solitude I needed to put my thoughts on paper without interruption. Oh what glorious times I had alone with my Father on those times away on the mountain. Many times I wanted to just stay in that solitude, but God had other plans.

I want to thank Scooter Watson who has spent hours editing the manuscript. God provided your expertise to help get this material into the hands of hurting families. Thank you for how you have allowed God to use you when you are in such a hard place yourself. God has worked through you in a mighty way to hopefully bless others.

Thank you Deborah Lalik as you helped me in the beginning of this writing process. To Ashley Harrison, Katy Hampton, and Bryan Lampley, who all helped me in the final stages with your computer skills. Thank you to Dee Dee Harrison for your generosity, without which this project could not have been completed. May God continue to pour out His blessings on you.

My gratitude to Sylvia Gunter, who also honored me by reading my manuscript, and giving me valuable suggestions. You helped me believe my writings could comfort someone else. Thank you for all the prayers that have blessed my life over the past few years from your own writings. Thank you for your blessing books that have allowed me to pray them over my family and friends as well as our ministry families.

Thanks to Kelli Benfield who contributed to the book cover design and to Lynda Hobson who did the photography on the back cover. I appreciate you both more than you know.

It is hard to put down on paper the people who have been so influential in your life and give them the credit they are due without leaving someone out. I want to say thank you to many of you who have prayed so long for our prodigal to return. You have been faithful to intercede and I pray God's continued blessings upon you.

Thank you to all the families who have allowed me to walk with you through the tough days you have faced with your prodigal loved one. It has been my privilege and honor.

Taken from Prayer Essentials II

Sylvia Gunter, Pages 156-157.

God gave the vision of the valley of dry bones to His prophet Jeremiah because the heart of the Father weeps over the dry bones of His people, as Jesus wept over the city of Jerusalem. I have prayed Ezekiel 37:1-14 for the dry bones of the church, and without exception that is how I have heard it preached. That is a valid picture of a powerful intercessory burden, because the Spirit of God wants to breathe new life into vast areas of spiritual dryness, barrenness, and deadness.

Not long ago, my heart cried with a friend for her wayward young prodigal. My sister-friend said, "We were in a new place for us of desperation of soul that could only squeak 'Jesus' or 'God, help me' or 'God, do something.' These are incredibly powerful squeaks because of the desperation that throws itself entirely on God." This is the cry from a parent's desperate heart for God to do what only God can do. I identified with the need of that family and prayed for the barrenness in that young life through Ezekiel's word picture in Ezekiel 37.

Ask for a weeping heart of mercy, not judgment, to carry the gift of discernment for repentance. Until you can put your tears and your life on the line for the person, marriage, family, church, city, or nation that needs revival, you are not in the position of having the heart and mind of Jesus for them. Open your Bible in Ezekiel 37 and read the verses, crying out to God for your own "dry bones: situations in your family.

Ezekiel 37

37:1 Father, Your hand is upon us in Spirit-led intercession for _____. Purify our hearts by Your Spirit and deposit Your burden of prayer in us, unmixed with unsanctified sympathies, anger, bitterness, or human judgments. We are trusting You to bring us through the valley of the shadow of death, as You promised. Lead us to pray as large, deep, and wide as Your providence in this situation. Give us a heart of wisdom and mercy that rejoices against judgment for _____.

37:2 We trust that You have gone before and are working, even when we don't see Your purposes. Spirit of the Lord, lead us to rightly discern the real condition of _____, not just react to what we think or have been told. You see the dry bones of barrenness and desolation. You know the entrances that _____ has given the kingdom of evil. _____ is oppressed, fragmented, miserable and unhappy, alienated from Your blessing, morally compromised with sin and deception, rebelling against their parents and Your Word, and in great danger. Their present condition is not hopeless to You. In darkness, You are light.

37:3 Spirit of counsel, You know everything. You don't need us to inform You of anything. You want from us restful, trusting communion and absolute surrender to Your will, Your ways, and Your timing. We humbly acknowledge our absolute dependence on You for faith to stand, for knowledge and counsel, for comfort and security, for direction and outcome. Let us speak only Your prayers. Let us not accept as final the circumstances of wickedness and iniquity that our eyes see. You alone know the end form the beginning, and You are the God of the impossible.

37:4 We say to deaf ears, "Hear the word of the Lord!" At Your direction, let us discern and pray Your purposes for _____ and the entire family. As we pray speak Your words to them and cause them to respond obediently to You. Enable us to pray Your prayers for the dry bones of _____'s body and soul (heart, mind, will, and emotions). Holy Spirit, call forth Your purposes and the future and hope that You have planned for _____.

37:5-6 Sovereign Lord, speak Your creative and restoring miracle to the barrenness in _____'s life with the same resurrection power that brought Jesus Christ to life from the dead. Breathe new life into them by Your Spirit. Set everything in place in working order in their life, so that _____ will know that You are Lord, Sovereign Ruler, rightfully due their loyalty and obedient service.

37:7 By faith, we believe You, obey You, and pray as You command. Answer by Your Spirit and open a way where there seems to be no way. You go before, the God of break-through. Give us a sign of encouragement. Let us hear the "rattling bones" coming together as You make _____ who You intend them to be---healthy, whole, functioning, life-giving. By Your blood, Lord Jesus, regenerate life in them and cause the marrow of their being to begin to sustain life.

37:8 Thank You for every sign of Your goodness we see, no matter how small. You are answering, and we ask You to do it thoroughly. Superficial answers, cleaning up their act, and looking functional are not enough! Stop short of nothing less than a new heart, a new spirit, a new life. Enable us to reach deeper into Your heart to pray. Your promises until Your full purposes are accomplished in all the family.

37:9 Sovereign Lord, call forth from the north, the south, the east, and the west the breath of life for _____. You formed them in their mother's womb, and as You breathed into their nostrils the fist breath of their life, breathe into them the new life of the Spirit in all Your favor and purpose. Restore them to wholeness. Speak to them, "Choose wisdom, choose righteousness, choose freedom, choose life!"

37:10-11 No situation is hopeless to You. Sovereign Lord, break off the shackles of captivity. Cause _____ to stand up in all the fullness of Your redeeming power. Make _____ mighty in the Spirit. Deliver them as an effectual weapon in Your hand. Set them into all Your spiritual gifts and calling among their generation of yet-to-be evangelists, preachers, disciplers, and world-changers that Satan is working overtime to annihilate. Let us see Your glory in these things that were intended for evil.

37:12 You have the keys to open the prison doors of sin, bondage, and the pit of destruction. Bring this captive out into all their true inheritance in You. Restore them to the family and the family of God.

37:13-14 Father, You have promised to give _____ Your spirit and new life, so that many will know that You have done it. Act in such a way that _____'s transformation will be a testimony to Your redemptive power. What You are doing, do quickly. In Jesus name, Amen.

In His Presence

You may be standing in a desperate situation in the battle of a lifetime. You may feel that you are in the darkest storm of your life. You may be the parent of an out-of-control child, and it seems that everything in your world is out of your control! Good news! It is! But God is still in control. El Roi, the God who sees knows it all and has a plan that He is working out. God will change your prodigal inside out, not just clean up his act. Take strength and comfort from these prayers. Re-center yourself on God's promises, and take up new prayer weapons to fight the real enemy, not the person.

BIBLIOGRAPHY

Quote by Lilias Trotter from Parables of the Cross, compiled and edited by Miriam Huffman Rockness, A Blossom in the Desert, (Discovery House distributed by Barbour Publishing, Inc., Uhrichsville, Ohio, 2007) pg. 1.

Chapter 1

1. Rick Warren, *The Purpose Driven Life* (Zondervan, Grand Rapids, Michigan, 49530, 2002), 29-30.

Chapter 2

1. Hinds Feet on High Places, Hannah Hurnard, Copyright © 1975 by Tyndale House Publishers, Inc.

Chapter 4

1. Excerpted from *Family News From Dr. James Dobson*, February 1996 edition Copyright© © 1996, 1-6, Focus on the Family, Colorado Springs, Colorado All rights reserved, used by permission "Oh! My Papa," English words by John Turner and Geoffrey Parsons, music and original lyrics by Paul Eurkhand. Copyright© 1948, 1950 Musikverlag und Buhnenvertrieb Zurich A.G., Zurich, Switzerland. Copyright© 1953 Shapiro, Bernstein & Co. Inc., New York. Copyright© Renewed. International Copyright© Secured. All rights Reserved. Used by Permission. "We're Not Gonna Take It," Twisted Sister, Copyright© 1984 Atlantic Records. "I Saw Your

Mommy," written by Mike Muir. Copyright© 1984 You'll Be Sorry Music, (BMI)/American Lesion Music (BMI). Administered by Bug Music. All Rights Reserved. Used by Permission.

2. "For All Who Knew the Shelter of the Fold," taken from Prodigals and Those Who Love Them, by Ruth Bell Graham, Baker Books, a division of Baker Publishing Group, © 1991, 15, "Used by Permission."

Chapter 5

1. Charles F. Stanley, Quote from In Touch Magazine.

2. Surviving the Prodigals in your Life, Woodrow Kroll, Back to the Bible Publishing, P.O. Box 82808, Lincoln, Nebraska, 68501, Copyright© 2001, 122-125. Used by permission.

Chapter 10

1. *The Conquest of Canaan* by Jessie Penn-Lewis, Copyright© 1992 by CLC Publications. Used by permissions of CLC Publications. May not be further reproduced. All rights reserved.

Chapter 11

1. Standing in the Gap Poem, unknown author.

Chapter 12

1. Jack Hayford, *Pastors Heart Newsletter, Whispers In The Dark,* (March/April, 2002).

Chapter 13

1. Dr. Dan B. Allender & Dr. Tremper Longman III, *Bold Love*, (Nav Press, Colorado Springs, Co 80935, 1992), 234-263. Used by permission.

Chapter 14

1. Quote from http://www.nida.nih.gov/infofacts/marijuana.html

2. Quote from http://www.health.org/govpubs/phd640i/

Chapter 18

1. Hinds Feet on High Places, Hannah Hurnard, copyright © 1975 by Tyndale House Publishers, Inc., 26.

Chapter 19

1. Jennifer Kennedy Dean, Setting Captives Free, praying for the unsaved, eBook, Copyright© 2005. 10, 17. Used by permission.

2. Jennifer Kennedy Dean, Legacy Of Prayer, (New Hope Publishers, Birmingham, AL, Copyright© 2002), pgs.73-91. Used by permission.

3. Henry Blackaby, Created to Be God's Friend; Lessons From The Life Of Abraham, (Published in Nashville, Tennessee, by Thomas Nelson, Inc., 1999),151. Copyright© 1999 by Henry T. Blackaby

Chapter 20

1. Beth Moore, *Believing God Workbook,* p. 69-70, (Broadman & Holman Publishers, Nashville, Tennessee, 2004).

2. The Devotional Classics of C.H. Spurgeon: Morning and Evening, A Book of Daily Devotions by C. H. Spurgeon, published by SOVEREIGN GRACE TRUST FUND, Lafayette, Indiana, 47903, 1990, p. 168.

Chapter 21

1.The Devotional Classics of C. H. Spurgeon, Morning and Evening, A Book of Daily Devotions, published by Sovereign Grace Trust Fund, Lafayette, Indiana 47903,1990, 230.

2. Words and Music by Anna Hutto and Connie Harrington. Copyright 1995 by BMG Songs, Inc. and B-B-Bryan Music (all rights reserved).

Chapter 22

1. Watchman Nee, The Release of the Spirit, Sure Foundation Publishers, Copyright© 1965, 13.

2. Copyright© 1988 by Gaviota Music (a dv. of Manna Music, Inc.), 35255 Brooten Road, Pacific City, OR 97135. All rights Reserved. Used by Permission. (BMI).

3. John MacArthur, A Tale of Two Sons (Nashville, Tennessee: 2008), 116-117. Used by permission.

4. Charles F. Stanley, March 2002 newsletter.

Poem by Sandra Pulliam written for On Wings Like a Dove in 2008.

Dry Bones Praying, taken from Prayer Essentials II by Sylvia Gunter, 156-157. Used by permission.

RECOMMENDED READING

Prodigals and Those Who Love Them, Ruth Bell Graham

As Silver Refined, Kay Arthur

Bringing Home The Prodigals, Rob Parsons

Anger: Handling A Powerful Emotion In A Healthy Way, Dr. Gary Chapman

Brokenness: How God Redeems Pain and Suffering, Lon Solomon

Will Your Prodigal Come Home?, Jeff Lucas

When I Lay My Isaac Down, Carol Kent

A New Kind Of Normal, Carol Kent

Parenting Your Adult Child, Dr. Gary Chapman and Ross Campbell, M. D.

A Tale Of Two Sons, Dr. John MacArthur

Praying for Your Prodigal Daughter, Janet Thompson

Can God be Trusted in Our Trials?, Tony Evans

Praying God's Word, Beth Moore

When Godly People do Ungodly Things, Beth Moore

Boundaries, Dr. Henry Cloud & Dr. John Townsend

LaVergne, TN USA
28 February 2011
218108LV00002B/3/P